# Great

## PUB FOOD

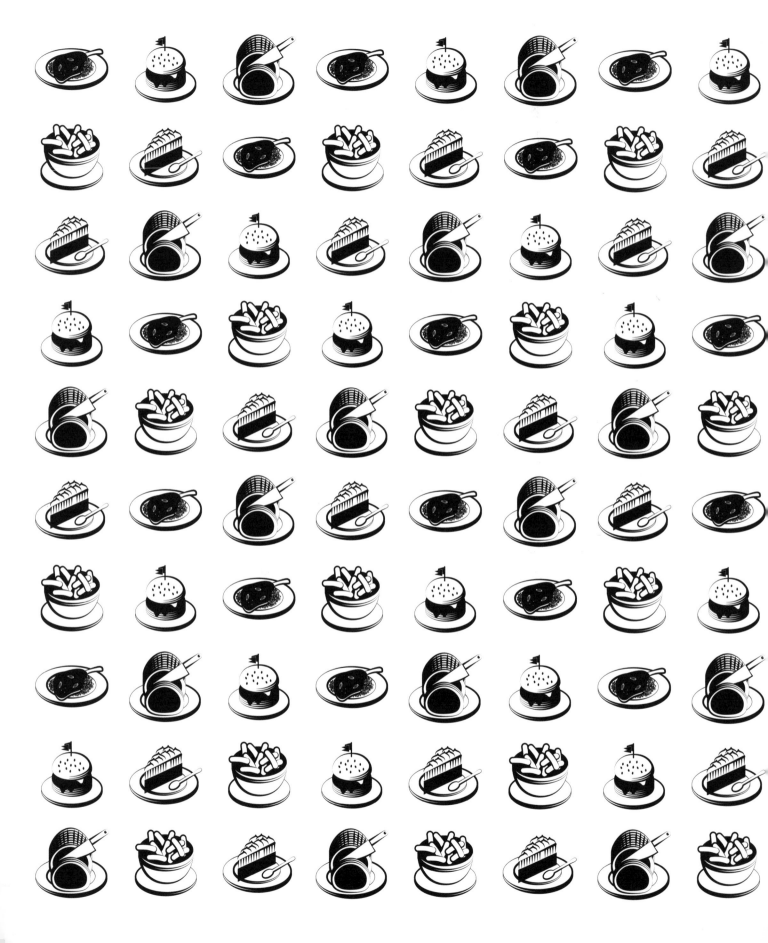

# MAKE HOME
## Great
## PUB FOOD
### YOUR NEW LOCAL

Rachael Lane

**hardie grant** books

MELBOURNE · LONDON

# Contents

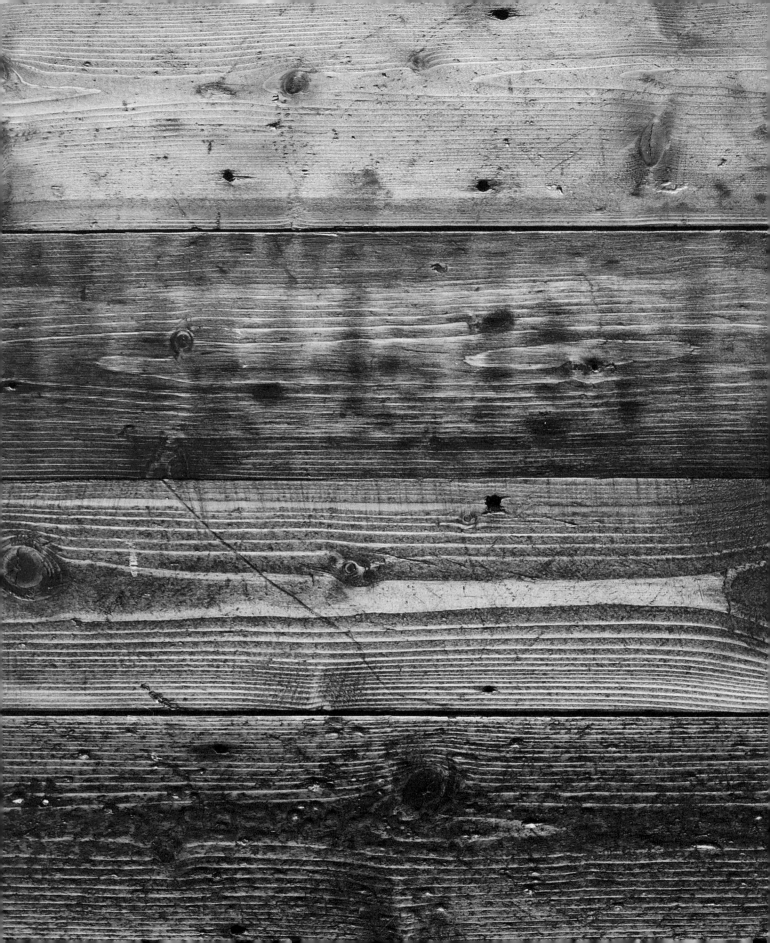

Tandoori Chicken
Burgers

Greek Lamb and
Haloumi Burgers

Tempura Fish Burgers
with Wasabi Mayo

Beef and Blue
Cheese Burgers

Pulled Pork Sliders
with Coleslaw
and Pickles

Lentil Vegie Burgers
with Peanut Sauce

Prawn Cocktail Rolls

Steak Sandwiches with
Caramelised Onion,
Smoked Cheddar
and Bacon

Gourmet Hotdogs with
Braised Red Cabbage
and Apple

Beef Burgundy Pie

Steak and
Mushroom Pie

Beef and
Guinness Pie

Chicken and
Tarragon Pie

Vegie Curry Pie

Shortcrust Pastry

Smoked Fish Pie

Shepherd's Pie

Pork Pies

Cornish Pasties

Vegetable Pasties

Pork and Fennel
Sausage Rolls

# — TANDOORI CHICKEN BURGERS —

**4 white sourdough burger buns**
**4 baby cos (romaine) lettuce leaves,**
**shredded**
**1 Lebanese (short) cucumber,**
**peeled lengthways into ribbons**
**½ avocado, sliced**
**½ red onion, thinly sliced**

### TANDOORI CHICKEN
**½ cup (125 g/4 oz) plain yoghurt**
**juice of ½ lemon**
**3 garlic cloves, crushed**
**2 teaspoons finely grated ginger**
**1 teaspoon ground cumin**
**1 teaspoon chilli powder**
**1 teaspoon ground coriander**
**½ teaspoon ground turmeric**
**2 chicken thigh fillets, halved**

### MANGO CHUTNEY
**1 large ripe mango, flesh coarsely**
**chopped**
**3 tablespoons cider vinegar**
**3 tablespoons soft brown sugar**
**2 cm (¾ in) piece ginger,**
**peeled and finely chopped**
**½ teaspoon cumin seeds**
**pinch of dried chilli flakes**

To prepare the tandoori chicken, combine the yoghurt, lemon juice, garlic, ginger and spices in a medium-sized bowl. Add the chicken thighs and toss to coat. Cover and refrigerate for at least 4 hours or overnight.

Meanwhile to make the chutney, combine all the ingredients in a small saucepan over low–medium heat and bring to the boil. Decrease the heat and gently simmer, stirring occasionally, for 20–25 minutes, until the mango is soft and the chutney thick. Transfer to a bowl and set aside to cool.

Preheat a griller (broiler) to high.

Preheat a flat grill plate or large frying pan over high heat. Cook the chicken thighs for 4 minutes on each side, or until cooked through and golden-brown.

Meanwhile cut the buns in half horizontally and toast the cut sides under the grill.

Arrange the cos leaves, cucumber, avocado and onion on the bun bases. Place the chicken on top, spoon on mango chutney, cover with the lids and serve.

☞ Mango chutney can be made in advance. Double the recipe to have at hand when required. Store in a sterilised glass bottle or jar in the refrigerator for up to 6 months.

# Greek Lamb and Haloumi Burgers

1 tablespoon olive oil
250 g (9 oz) haloumi, cut into 4 slices
4 small Turkish rolls or crusty square rolls
4 baby cos (romaine) lettuce leaves, torn

### Burgers
600 g (1 lb 5 oz) minced (ground) lamb
½ small red onion, finely chopped
2 garlic cloves, crushed
2 tablespoons finely chopped oregano
2 tablespoons finely chopped mint
sea salt and freshly ground black pepper

### Tzatziki
½ cup (125 g/4 oz) Greek-style yoghurt
½ Lebanese (short) cucumber,
  deseeded and finely diced
1 tablespoon finely chopped mint
1 tablespoon lemon juice
1 garlic clove, crushed

### Greek-style Salsa
2 vine-ripened tomatoes, finely diced
¼ red onion, finely diced
⅓ cup (50 g/1¾ oz) pitted kalamata olives,
  coarsely chopped
2 tablespoons chopped flat-leaf
  (Italian) parsley
2 teaspoons extra-virgin olive oil
2 teaspoons lemon juice
1 teaspoon dried oregano
freshly ground black pepper

To make the burgers, combine the lamb, onion, garlic, oregano and mint in a medium-sized bowl. Season with salt and pepper. Shape into 4 even-sized patties. Put on a plate, cover and refrigerate for 30 minutes.

Meanwhile, to make the tzatziki, combine the yoghurt, cucumber, mint, lemon juice and garlic in a small bowl.

To make the salsa, combine the tomato, onion, olives and parsley in a small bowl. Add the olive oil, lemon juice and oregano and stir to combine. Season with freshly ground black pepper.

Preheat a griller (broiler) to high.

Preheat a flat grill plate or large frying pan over medium heat. Drizzle with oil and cook the burgers for 4 minutes on each side, for medium, or until cooked to your liking. Cook the haloumi for 30 seconds on each side, or until golden-brown.

Cut the rolls in half horizontally and toast the cut sides under the grill.

Arrange the cos leaves and salsa on the roll bases. Place the burgers and haloumi on top, spoon on tzatziki, cover with the lids and serve.

# — Tempura Fish Burgers —
# — with Wasabi Mayo —

4 × 150 g (5 oz) skinless and boneless
  firm white fish fillets, such as
  barramundi or blue-eye
4 floured bap buns
2 large handfuls watercress,
  leaves picked
1 carrot, halved and cut into thin strips
½ avocado, sliced
2 large handfuls snow pea (mangetout)
  sprouts, trimmed

### Wasabi Mayo
1 large egg yolk
2 teaspoons wasabi paste
2 tablespoons lemon juice
½ cup (125 ml/4 fl oz) light olive oil
sea salt

### Tempura Batter
1 cup (250 ml/8½ fl oz) chilled soda water
3 ice cubes
1 large egg yolk
¾ cup (110 g/3¾ oz)
  plain (all-purpose) flour
3 tablespoons cornflour (cornstarch)

To make the wasabi mayo, whisk the egg yolk, wasabi paste and lemon juice together in a small bowl. Gradually pour in the oil, whisking continuously, until thick. Season with salt.

To make the tempura batter, combine the soda water, ice cubes and egg yolk in a medium-sized bowl. Sift in the flours. Stir using chopsticks, until just combined; the batter should be slightly lumpy.

Two-thirds fill a deep-fryer or a large heavy-based saucepan with vegetable oil and heat to 190°C (375°F). Place a wire rack on a baking tray, for draining.

Preheat a griller (broiler) to high.

Dredge the fish through the tempura batter and fry, 2 pieces at a time, for 3–4 minutes, until crisp and light golden. Transfer to the wire rack to drain.

Meanwhile cut the buns in half horizontally and toast the cut sides under the grill.

Arrange the watercress, carrot and snow pea sprouts on the bun bases. Place the fish and avocado on top, spoon on some wasabi mayo, cover with the lids and serve.

# — BEEF AND BLUE CHEESE BURGERS —

**MAKES 4**

200 g (7 oz) blue-vein cheese, crumbled
4 brioche buns
2 large handfuls rocket (arugula)
2 vine-ripened tomatoes,
    sliced into rounds
2 dill-pickle cucumbers,
    sliced lengthways

### BURGERS

300 g (10 oz) minced (ground) beef
300 g (10 oz) minced (ground) pork
$\frac{1}{2}$ brown onion, coarsely grated
1 tablespoon Worcestershire sauce
sea salt and freshly ground black pepper

### BARBECUE SAUCE

1 cup (250 ml/8$\frac{1}{2}$ fl oz) passata (pureed
    tomatoes)
3 tablespoons molasses
2 tablespoons malt vinegar
2 tablespoons maple syrup
1 tablespoon Worcestershire sauce
1 chipotle chilli in adobo sauce,
    finely chopped (optional)
2 teaspoons dijon mustard
$\frac{1}{2}$ teaspoon ground cumin
$\frac{1}{4}$ teaspoon smoked paprika
sea salt and freshly ground black pepper

To make the burgers, combine the beef and pork, onion and Worcestershire sauce in a medium-sized bowl. Season with salt and pepper. Shape into 4 even-sized burgers. Put on a plate, cover and refrigerate for 30 minutes.

To make the barbecue sauce, combine all the ingredients except salt and pepper in a small saucepan over medium heat and bring to the boil. Decrease the heat and simmer for 10 minutes or until the sauce thickens. Season with salt and pepper. Transfer to a bowl and set aside to cool.

Preheat a griller (broiler) to high.

Preheat a flat grill plate or large frying pan over medium heat. Drizzle with oil and cook the burgers for 4 minutes on each side, for medium, or until cooked to your liking.

Meanwhile cut the buns in half horizontally and toast the cut sides under the grill.

Transfer the burgers onto a tray small enough to fit under the grill. Place the blue cheese on top of the burgers and melt under the grill.

Arrange the rocket and tomato on the bun bases. Place the burgers with blue cheese and a few slices of pickled cucumbers on top. Spoon on the barbecue sauce, cover with the lids and serve.

☞ Barbecue sauce can be made in advance. Double the recipe to have at hand when required. Store in a sterilised glass bottle or jar in the refrigerator for up to 6 months.

# Pulled Pork Sliders with
# Coleslaw and Pickles

**SERVES 4**

8 dinner rolls
whole-egg mayonnaise, for spreading
4 dill-pickle cucumbers, sliced

## Pulled Pork
2 tablespoons olive oil
600 g (1 lb 5 oz) boneless pork shoulder
2 teaspoons mild smoked paprika
1 teaspoon dried chilli flakes
1 teaspoon ground cumin
½ cup (125 ml/4 fl oz) chicken stock
finely grated zest and juice of 1 orange
3 tablespoons soft brown sugar
2 tablespoons cider vinegar
2 tablespoons tomato ketchup
1 tablespoon Worcestershire sauce
2 garlic cloves, crushed
2 cm (¾ in) piece ginger,
    peeled and finely grated

## Coleslaw
2 cups (150 g/5 oz) finely shredded red
    cabbage
½ carrot, grated
1 large handful coriander (cilantro)
juice of 1 lime
1 tablespoon maple syrup
2 tablespoons olive oil

To prepare the pulled pork, heat the oil in a heavy-based saucepan over medium–high heat. Coat the pork in the paprika, chilli and cumin. Cook the pork for 4–5 minutes, or until browned all over. Add the chicken stock, orange zest and juice, sugar, vinegar, tomato ketchup, Worcestershire sauce, garlic and ginger to the pan and bring to the boil. Decrease the heat, cover and gently simmer for 1½ hours, or until tender. Remove the pork from the liquid and set aside on a plate to cool slightly.

Simmer the liquid over medium heat, for 5–10 minutes, until reduced to make a thick sauce. Shred the pork, add to the sauce and stir to coat.

To prepare the coleslaw, combine the cabbage, carrot and coriander in a medium-sized bowl. Combine the lime juice, maple syrup and olive oil in a small bowl. Pour over the coleslaw and toss to coat.

Cut the rolls in half horizontally and spread the mayonnaise on the lids. Divide the pulled pork between the bases, top with coleslaw and cover with the lids.

Serve 2 sliders per person with dill pickles alongside.

# Lentil Vegie Burgers — with Peanut Sauce —

1 tablespoon olive oil
4 crusty wholegrain burger buns
2 large handfuls baby spinach
1 Lebanese (short) cucumber, sliced
2 vine-ripened tomatoes, sliced
½ red onion, sliced
chilli sauce (optional)

### Burgers

¾ cup (140 g/5 oz) brown lentils
¾ cup (185 g/6 oz) red lentils
2 tablespoons olive oil
1 small onion, finely chopped
2 garlic cloves, finely chopped
2 cm (¾ in) piece ginger,
   peeled and finely chopped
1 small red chilli, deseeded and
   finely chopped
1 carrot, coarsely grated
1 zucchini (courgette), coarsely grated
2 teaspoons ground cumin
1 teaspoon ground coriander
1 cup (80 g/2½ oz) fresh breadcrumbs
1 large handful coriander (cilantro)
   leaves, chopped
1 tablespoon tahini
1 tablespoon lemon juice
sea salt and freshly ground black pepper

### Peanut Sauce

1 tablespoon peanut oil
1 French shallot, finely chopped
2 garlic cloves, finely chopped
2 cm (¾ in) piece ginger, peeled and
   finely grated
1 small red chilli, deseeded and
   finely chopped
½ cup (125 g/4 oz) crunchy peanut butter
1 × 270 ml (9½ fl oz) tin coconut milk
juice of 1 lime
1 tablespoon soy sauce
1 tablespoon soft brown sugar

To make the burgers, put the brown and red lentils in separate saucepans, cover with cold water and bring to the boil. Decrease the heat and simmer the brown lentils for 15 minutes and the red lentils for 5 minutes or until tender. Strain and transfer both to a medium-sized bowl.

Heat the oil in a large frying pan over low–medium heat. Cook the onion, garlic, ginger and chilli until softened. Add the carrot, zucchini and spices and cook for 5 minutes, until the carrot has softened and spices are fragrant.

Add the cooked vegetables, breadcrumbs, coriander, tahini and lemon juice to the lentils and stir to combine. Season with salt and pepper. Shape into 4 even-sized burgers. Put on a plate, cover and refrigerate for 30 minutes.

Meanwhile, to make the peanut sauce, heat the oil in a small saucepan over low–medium heat. Cook the shallot, garlic, ginger and chilli until softened. Add the peanut butter, coconut milk, lime juice, soy sauce and sugar, and stir to combine. Simmer for 2 minutes or until the sugar has dissolved.

Preheat a griller (broiler) to high.

Preheat a flat grill plate or large frying pan over medium heat. Drizzle with oil and cook the burgers for 4 minutes on each side, or until golden-brown.

Meanwhile cut the buns in half horizontally and toast the cut sides under the grill.

Arrange the spinach, cucumber, tomato and red onion on the bun bases and place the burgers on top. Add chilli sauce (if desired) and peanut sauce. Cover with the lids and serve.

# — PRAWN COCKTAIL ROLLS —

24 cooked peeled prawns (shrimp)
½ small red onion, finely diced
1 long sourdough baguette,
    cut into 4 lengths
4 iceberg lettuce leaves, shredded
1 avocado, sliced
1 Lebanese (short) cucumber, peeled
    lengthways into ribbons

COCKTAIL SAUCE
1 large egg yolk
1 teaspoon dijon mustard
1 tablespoon white wine vinegar
½ cup (125 ml/4 fl oz) light olive oil
1 tablespoon tomato ketchup
2 teaspoons Worcestershire sauce
dash of Tabasco sauce, or to taste
sea salt and ground white pepper

To make the cocktail sauce, whisk the egg yolk, mustard and vinegar together in a small bowl. Gradually pour in the oil, whisking continuously, until thick. Stir in the tomato, Worcestershire and Tabasco sauces. Season with salt and white pepper.

Coarsely chop half of the prawns and place in a medium-sized bowl. Add 3 tablespoons of the cocktail sauce and the red onion, and stir to combine.

Cut the baguette quarters in half horizontally but not all the way through, so the bread stays joined like a roll. Cover the bases with lettuce, avocado and cucumber. Divide the prawn mixture evenly between the rolls and top each one with the remaining prawns, an additional dollop of sauce and pepper.

Serve.

# Steak Sandwiches with Caramelised Onion, Smoked Cheddar and Bacon

8 short slices bacon
4 × 150 g (5 oz) sirloin steaks
olive oil, for drizzling
sea salt and freshly ground black pepper
8 slices smoked cheddar
8 slices sourdough bread
½ cup (125 ml/4 fl oz)
   whole-egg mayonnaise
Barbecue Sauce (page 12)
2 large handfuls rocket (arugula)

### Caramelised Onion
1 tablespoon olive oil
20 g (¾ oz) butter
3 brown onions, thinly sliced
2 tablespoons soft brown sugar
1 tablespoon malt vinegar

To make the caramelised onion, heat the oil and butter in a frying pan over low heat. Add the onion and cook, stirring occasionally, for 15 minutes or until softened. Add the sugar and vinegar and cook for a further 10–15 minutes, or until caramelised. Transfer to a small bowl and set aside.

Preheat a griller (broiler) to high.

Preheat a char-grill or large frying pan over medium–high heat. Cook the bacon for 1–2 minutes on each side, or until golden-brown. Transfer to paper towel to drain.

Put steaks between two sheets of baking paper and gently flatten with a rolling pin or meat mallet.

Increase the heat to high. Drizzle the steaks with olive oil and season with salt and pepper. Cook for 1 minute on each side for medium–rare or until cooked to your liking. Transfer the steaks onto a tray small enough to fit under the grill. Place slices of smoked cheddar on top and melt under the grill. Remove the steaks and set aside. Lightly toast the bread slices under the griller.

Spread the mayonnaise over all of the bread slices. On 4 of the slices place a steak with cheese and top with bacon. Spoon on some barbecue sauce followed by caramelised onions and rocket. Cover with the remaining bread and serve.

# — Gourmet Hotdogs with — Braised Red Cabbage and Apple —

4 bratwurst sausages
4 soft long rolls
dijon mustard, to serve
1 cup (125 g/4 oz) grated cheddar

### Braised Red Cabbage and Apple
1 tablespoon olive oil
20 g (³/₄ oz) butter
1 red onion, thinly sliced
1 garlic clove, finely chopped
¹/₂ teaspoon caraway seeds
1 bay leaf
¹/₄ red cabbage, shredded
3 tablespoons apple juice
1 tablespoon apple cider vinegar
1 large granny smith apple peeled,
   cored and coarsely grated
1 small handful flat-leaf (Italian)
   parsley, chopped

To make the braised red cabbage and apple, heat the oil and butter in a saucepan over low–medium heat. Cook the onion and garlic, until softened. Add the caraway seeds and bay leaf and cook until fragrant. Add the cabbage and cook, stirring occasionally, for 5 minutes or until it begins to soften. Pour in the apple juice and vinegar, cover and cook for 10 minutes. Add the apple, cover and cook for a further 5 minutes, or until the apple has softened and the liquid has reduced. Add the parsley and stir to combine. Transfer to a medium-sized bowl and set aside.

Preheat a griller (broiler) to high.

Preheat a char-grill or large frying pan over medium heat. Cook the sausages, turning frequently, for 5–7 minutes or until golden-brown and cooked through.

Cut the rolls down the centre lengthways, but do not cut all the way through. Spread mustard on the rolls, fill with cabbage and sausages. Sprinkle with cheese and melt it slightly under the grill, if desired.

Serve.

# BEEF BURGUNDY PIE

1 quantity Shortcrust Pastry (page 28)
1–3 sheets frozen puff pastry, thawed
   (you will require more for individual pies)
1 large egg, lightly beaten, for glazing

FILLING
40 g (1½ oz) butter
10 French shallots, quartered
2 celery stalks, diced
5 garlic cloves, finely chopped
1.2 kg (2 lb 10 oz) beef shin,
   (sinew trimmed and discarded)
   cut into 2.5 cm (1 in) chunks
3 tablespoons plain (all-purpose) flour
sea salt and freshly ground black pepper
3 tablespoons olive oil
750 ml (25 fl oz) full-bodied red wine, such
   as shiraz or merlot
1 cup (250 ml/8½ fl oz) beef stock
2 bay leaves
6 sprigs thyme

Melt the butter in a wide heavy-based saucepan over low–medium heat. Add the shallots, celery and garlic and cook until softened. Set aside in a bowl.

Toss the beef in flour seasoned with salt and pepper. Add a little of the oil to the saucepan and adjust the heat to high. Brown the beef in batches, adding oil each time. Return the vegetable mix to the pan and pour in the wine and beef stock. Add the bay leaves and thyme and stir to combine. Cover and gently simmer over low heat for 1½ hours. Uncover and simmer for a further 30 minutes or until the meat is tender and the sauce has thickened.

Preheat the oven to 200°C (400°F/ Gas 6).

Transfer the stew into a bowl and set aside for 20 minutes, to cool slightly.

Meanwhile, cut the pie top/s out of the puff pastry, using the pie tins or dish to make the correct size. Lay the pastry flat on a tray and refrigerate until required.

Grease the pie dishes: six 1 cup (250 ml/8½ fl oz) individual tins or one 4 cm (1½ in) deep, 28 cm × 25 cm (11 in × 10 in) pie dish. Line the dishes with the shortcrust pastry.

Fill the pie base/s with stew, discarding the thyme sprigs and bay leaves. Moisten the edges with water and cover with the puff pastry tops. Press around the edges with your thumb or a fork to seal. Cut a few slits in the pastry top/s, to allow the steam to escape. Brush with egg.

Place the pie/s on a baking tray and bake for 20–30 minutes, if individual pies, or 40 minutes for a large pie, or until the top is puffed and golden-brown.

# STEAK AND MUSHROOM PIE

1 quantity Shortcrust Pastry (page 28)
1–3 sheets frozen puff pastry, thawed
  (you will require more for individual pies)
1 large egg, lightly beaten, for glazing

FILLING
40 g (1½ oz) butter
1 onion, diced
4 garlic cloves, finely chopped
500 g (1 lb 2 oz) mixed mushrooms, such
  as Swiss brown and pine, thickly sliced
1 kg (2 lb 3 oz) beef skirt steak
  (approximately 2 pieces) cut into
  2.5 cm (1 in) chunks
3 tablespoons plain (all-purpose) flour
sea salt and freshly ground black pepper
3 tablespoons olive oil
1 cup (250 ml/8½ fl oz) full-bodied
  red wine, such as shiraz or merlot
3 cups (750 ml/25 fl oz) beef stock
2 bay leaves
4 sprigs thyme

Melt the butter in a wide heavy-based saucepan over low–medium heat. Add the onion and garlic and cook until softened. Add the mushrooms and cook until golden-brown. Transfer to a bowl and set aside.

Toss the beef in flour seasoned with salt and pepper.

Add a little of the oil to the saucepan and adjust the heat to high. Brown the beef in batches, adding additional oil each time. Return the mushroom mix to the pan and pour in the wine and beef stock. Add the bay leaves and thyme and stir to combine. Cover and gently simmer over low heat for 1½ hours. Uncover and simmer for a further 30 minutes, or until the meat is tender and the sauce has thickened.

Preheat the oven to 200°C (400°F/Gas 6).

Transfer the beef stew into a bowl and set aside for 20 minutes, to cool slightly.

Meanwhile, cut the pie top/s out of the puff pastry, using the pie tins or dish to make the correct size. Lay the pastry flat on a tray and refrigerate until required.

Grease the pie dishes: six 1 cup (250 ml/8½ fl oz) individual tins or one 4 cm (1½ in) deep, 28 cm × 25 cm (11 in × 10 in) pie dish. Line the dishes with the shortcrust pastry.

Fill the pie base/s with filling, discarding the thyme sprigs and bay leaves. Moisten the edges with water and cover with the puff pastry tops. Press around the edges with your thumb or a fork to seal. Cut a few slits in the pastry top/s, to allow the steam to escape. Brush with egg.

Place the pie/s on a baking tray and bake for 20–30 minutes, if individual pies, or 40 minutes for a large pie, or until the top is puffed and golden-brown.

# — BEEF AND GUINNESS PIE —

1 quantity Shortcrust Pastry (page 28)
1–3 sheets frozen puff pastry, thawed
  (you will require more for individual pies)
1 large egg, lightly beaten, for glazing

FILLING
40 g (1½ oz) butter
2 onions, diced
2 celery stalks, diced
1 carrot, diced
5 garlic cloves, finely chopped
1.2 kg (2 lb 10 oz) beef shoulder
  (sinew trimmed and discarded),
  cut into 2.5 cm (1 in) chunks
3 tablespoons plain (all-purpose) flour
sea salt and freshly ground black pepper
3 tablespoons olive oil
2 × 440 ml (15 fl oz) cans Guinness beer
½ cup (125 ml/4 fl oz) beef stock
2 tablespoons Worcestershire sauce
1 tablespoon tomato paste
  (concentrated tomato purée)
1 sprig rosemary

Melt the butter in a wide heavy-based saucepan over low–medium heat. Add the onion, celery, carrot and garlic and cook until softened. Transfer to a bowl and set aside.

Toss the beef in flour seasoned with salt and pepper.

Add a little of the oil to the saucepan and adjust the heat to high. Brown the beef in batches, adding additional oil each time. Return the softened vegetable mix to the pan and pour in the Guinness and beef stock. Add the Worcestershire sauce, tomato paste and rosemary and stir to combine. Cover and gently simmer over low heat for 1½ hours. Uncover and simmer for a further 30 minutes, or until the meat is tender and the sauce has thickened.

Transfer the beef stew into a bowl and set aside for 20 minutes, to cool slightly.

Preheat the oven to 200°C (400°F/Gas 6).

Meanwhile, cut the pie top/s out of the puff pastry, using the pie tins or dish to make the correct size. Lay the pastry flat on a tray and refrigerate until required.

Grease the pie dishes: six 1 cup (250 ml/8½ fl oz) individual tins or one 4 cm (1½ in) deep, 28 cm × 25 cm (11 in × 10 in) pie dish. Line the dishes with the shortcrust pastry.

Fill the pie base/s with filling, discarding the rosemary. Moisten the edges with water and cover with the puff pastry tops. Press around the edges with your thumb or a fork to seal. Cut a few slits in the pastry top/s, to allow the steam to escape. Brush with egg.

Place the pie/s on a baking tray and bake for 20–30 minutes, if individual pies, or 40 minutes for a large pie, or until the top is puffed and golden-brown.

# — CHICKEN AND TARRAGON PIE —

1 quantity Shortcrust Pastry (page 28)
1–3 sheets frozen puff pastry, thawed
  (you will require more for individual pies)
1 large egg, lightly beaten, for glazing

FILLING
40 g (1½ oz) butter
1 onion, diced
½ leek, white part only, thinly sliced
4 garlic cloves, finely chopped
1.2 kg (2 lb 10 oz) skinless chicken thigh
  fillets, cut into 2.5 cm (1 in) chunks
3 tablespoons plain (all-purpose) flour
sea salt and freshly ground black pepper
3 tablespoons olive oil
½ cup (125 ml/4 fl oz) dry white wine
2 cups (500 ml/17 fl oz) chicken stock
1 cup (250 ml/8½ fl oz) pouring
  (whipping) cream
3 tablespoons tarragon, chopped

To prepare the filling, melt the butter in a wide heavy-based saucepan over low–medium heat. Add the onion, leek and garlic and cook until softened. Transfer to a bowl and set aside. Toss the chicken in flour seasoned with salt and pepper. Add a little of the oil to the saucepan and adjust the heat to high. Brown the chicken in batches, adding additional oil each time. Return the onion and leek mix to the pan. Pour in the wine and bring to the boil. Add the chicken stock and cream and simmer over low heat for 30 minutes. Add the tarragon and simmer for a further 10–15 minutes, or until the sauce has thickened.

Transfer the chicken stew into a bowl and set aside for 20 minutes, to cool slightly.

Preheat the oven to 200°C (400°F/ Gas 6).

Meanwhile, cut the pie top/s out of the puff pastry, using the pie tins or dish to make the correct size. Lay the pastry flat on a tray and refrigerate until required.

Grease the pie dishes: six 1 cup (250 ml/8½ fl oz) individual tins or one 4 cm (1½ in) deep, 28 cm × 25 cm (11 in × 10 in) pie dish. Line the dishes with the shortcrust pastry.

Fill the pie base/s with filling. Moisten the edges with water and cover with the puff pastry tops. Press around the edges with your thumb or a fork to seal. Cut a few slits in the pastry top/s, to allow the steam to escape. Brush with egg.

Place the pie/s on a baking tray and bake for 20–30 minutes, if individual pies, or 40 minutes for a large pie, or until the top is puffed and golden-brown.

# — VEGIE CURRY PIE —

**1 quantity Shortcrust Pastry (page 28)**
**1–3 sheets frozen puff pastry, thawed**
  **(you will require more for individual pies)**
**1 large egg, lightly beaten, for glazing**

FILLING
**1 tablespoon vegetable oil**
**1 onion, diced**
**2 garlic cloves, finely chopped**
**1 tablespoon finely grated ginger**
**1 long red chilli, deseeded and**
  **finely chopped**
**1½ tablespoons plain (all-purpose) flour**
**1 teaspoon garam masala**
**1 teaspoon ground cumin**
**1 teaspoon ground coriander**
**½ teaspoon ground turmeric**
**¼ teaspoon ground chilli**
**250 g (9 oz) cauliflower,**
  **cut into very small florets**
**1 carrot, cut into 1.5 cm (⅝ in) dice**
**1 potato, cut into 1.5 cm (⅝ in) dice**
**½ sweet potato,**
  **cut into 1.5 cm (⅝ in) dice**
**2 tomatoes, diced**
**80 g (3 oz) spinach, coarsely chopped**
**½ cup (60 g/2 oz) peas**
**½ cup (125 ml/4 fl oz) pouring**
  **(whipping) cream**
**sea salt and freshly ground black pepper**

To prepare the filling, heat the oil in a large frying pan over low–medium heat. Cook the onion, garlic, ginger and chilli until softened. Add the flour and spices and cook for 10 seconds, or until fragrant. Add the cauliflower, carrot, potato, sweet potato and 1 cup (250 ml/8½ fl oz) water. Cover and cook for 15 minutes until the liquid has reduced and the vegetables are tender. Add the tomato, spinach, peas and cream, and stir to combine. Cook, uncovered for a further 5 minutes, or until the sauce has thickened. Season with salt and pepper. Transfer to a bowl and set aside for 20 minutes, to cool slightly. Refrigerate until cold.

Preheat the oven to 200°C (400°F/ Gas 6).

Meanwhile, cut the pie top/s out of the puff pastry, using the pie tins or dish to make the correct size. Lay the pastry flat on a tray and refrigerate until required.

Grease the pie dishes: six 1 cup (250 ml/8½ fl oz) individual tins or one 4 cm (1½ in) deep, 28 cm × 25 cm (11 in × 10 in) pie dish. Line the dishes with the shortcrust pastry.

Fill the pie base/s with filling. Moisten the edges with water and cover with the puff pastry top/s. Press around the edges with your thumb or a fork to seal. Cut 4 slits in the pastry top/s, to allow the steam to escape. Brush with egg.

Place the pie/s on a baking tray and bake for 20–30 minutes, if individual pies, or 40 minutes if cooking a large pie, or until the top is puffed and golden-brown.

# SHORTCRUST PASTRY

2 cups (300 g/10½ oz) plain
  (all-purpose) flour
150 g (5 oz) chilled butter, cubed,
  plus melted butter, for greasing

Lightly grease six 1 cup (250 ml/8½ fl oz) individual pie tins or one 4 cm (1½ in) deep, 28 cm × 25 cm (11 in × 10 in) pie dish with melted butter. Refrigerate.

Place the flour and butter in a food processor and pulse, until the mixture resembles fine crumbs. Gradually add ⅓ cup (80 ml/3 fl oz) chilled water, pulsing to incorporate: the mix will look dry and crumbly. Turn onto a clean work surface, gently knead and shape into a disc. Do not overwork. Wrap in plastic wrap and refrigerate for 30 minutes. Alternatively, to make the dough by hand, rub the butter into the flour in a medium-sized bowl and mix in the water.

For individual pies, divide the pastry into six equal portions and roll each out between two sheets of baking paper, to about 3 mm (⅛ in) thick. For a large pie, roll out the entire pastry disc to a circle just larger than the pie dish. You should have a little pastry left over. Line the cold tins or dish with pastry and trim the excess. Refrigerate for 20 minutes.

☞ Pastry can be made in advance and frozen until required. Bring back to room temperature before rolling.

# SMOKED FISH PIE

**MAKES FOUR INDIVIDUAL PIES OR ONE LARGE PIE**

### FILLING

2 cups (500 ml/17 fl oz) milk

½ onion, studded with 3 whole cloves

2 bay leaves

4 black peppercorns

400 g (14 oz) skinless and boneless
firm white fish fillets, such as blue-eye
or trevally

20 g (¾ oz) butter

1 tablespoon olive oil

2 celery stalks, diced

½ leek, white part only, thinly sliced

2 spring onions (scallions), chopped

3 tablespoons plain (all-purpose) flour

1 smoked trout, about 300 g (10½ oz),
skin and bones removed, flesh flaked

3 large eggs, hard-boiled,
peeled and cut into wedges

½ cup (60 g/2 oz) frozen peas

1 tablespoon lemon juice

2 tablespoons chopped dill

2 tablespoons chopped
flat-leaf (Italian) parsley

1 tablespoon capers, rinsed and chopped

sea salt and freshly ground black pepper

### BREADCRUMB TOPPING

3 cups hand-torn white breadcrumbs

40 g (1½ oz) butter, melted

2 tablespoons chopped
flat-leaf (Italian) parsley

Combine the milk, onion, bay leaves and peppercorns in a saucepan and bring to the boil over high heat. Decrease the heat to a simmer, add the fish and poach for 5 minutes, or until it is just cooked through and flakes easily.

Remove the fish using a slotted spoon and transfer to a bowl. Flake the meat into chunks and set aside. Strain and reserve the poaching liquid.

Melt the butter and oil in a saucepan over low–medium heat. Cook the celery, leek and spring onion, until softened. Add the flour and cook, stirring, for 1 minute. Gradually pour in the reserved poaching liquid, stirring constantly to prevent lumps. Gently simmer, stirring constantly, for 5 minutes, or until the sauce thickens. Remove from the heat and add the flaked white fish, smoked trout, eggs, peas, lemon juice, dill, parsley and capers and stir to combine. Season with salt and pepper. Transfer to a bowl and set aside for 20 minutes, to cool slightly.

Preheat the oven to 200°C (400°F/ Gas 6).

Spoon the filling into four 1½ cup (375 ml/12½ fl oz) individual ovenproof ramekins or one 2 litre (64 fl oz) capacity ovenproof dish). Place the torn bread, butter and parsley in a medium-sized bowl and toss to combine. Sprinkle the breadcrumb topping over the filling.

Place the pie/s on a baking tray and bake for 15 minutes if individual pies, or 20–25 minutes if a large pie, or until the top is crunchy and golden.

# ● — SHEPHERD'S PIE — ●

### FILLING

**10 g (³/₈ oz) dried porcini mushrooms**
**1 tablespoon olive oil**
**2 onions, finely diced**
**2 carrots, finely diced**
**3 garlic cloves, finely chopped**
**700 g (1 lb 9 oz) minced (ground) lamb**
**¹/₂ cup (125 ml/4 fl oz) red wine**
**1 cup (250 ml/8¹/₂ fl oz) beef stock**
**2 tablespoons tomato paste**
  **(concentrated tomato purée)**
**2 tablespoons Worcestershire sauce**
**2 bay leaves**

### MASHED POTATO TOPPING

**1 kg (2 lb 3 oz) all-purpose potatoes,**
  **such as sebago or desiree**
**¹/₂ cup (125 ml/4 fl oz) pouring (whipping)**
  **cream**
**100 g (3¹/₂ oz) butter**
**1 teaspoon hot English mustard**
**sea salt and ground white pepper**
**1 cup (125 g/4 oz) grated cheddar**

To prepare the filling, soak the porcini mushrooms in ¹/₂ cup (125 ml/4 fl oz) hot water for 20 minutes, or until softened. Drain and coarsely chop.

Heat the oil in a heavy-based saucepan over low–medium heat. Cook the onion, carrot and garlic, until softened. Add the lamb and cook for 5–10 minutes, until browned. Pour in the wine and stock. Add the tomato paste, mushrooms, Worcestershire sauce and bay leaves and bring to the boil. Decrease the heat, cover and simmer for 30 minutes. Uncover and simmer for a further 15 minutes or until the meat is tender and the sauce is thick.

Meanwhile to make the mashed potato topping, peel and halve the potatoes and place in a large saucepan of cold salted water. Cover and bring to the boil over high heat. Uncover and boil for 15 minutes, or until tender when tested with a skewer. Drain.

Heat the cream, butter and mustard together in the saucepan over medium heat, until the butter has melted and the cream is hot. Return the potato to the pan and mash using a potato masher. Beat with a wooden spoon, to combine with the cream. Season with salt and white pepper.

Preheat the oven to 180°C (350°F/ Gas 4).

Spoon the filling into six 1¹/₂ cup (375 ml/12¹/₂ fl oz) capacity individual ovenproof ramekins or one 2 L (64 fl oz) capacity ovenproof dish and top with mashed potato and grated cheese.

Place the pie/s on a baking tray and bake for 15 minutes, if individual pies, or 20–25 minutes if cooking a large pie, or until the top is golden.

# — Pork Pies —

**MAKES 6**

### Filling
500 g (1 lb 2 oz) boned pork shoulder
2 slices bacon, coarsely chopped
1 tablespoon finely chopped  sage
1 tablespoon chopped thyme
½ teaspoon ground nutmeg
¼ teaspoon ground allspice
sea salt and freshly ground black pepper

### Hot Water Pastry
3 cups (450 g/1 lb) plain (all-purpose) flour
1 large egg, lightly beaten, plus
   1 large egg, lightly beaten, for glazing
100 g (3½ oz) lard, shortening or butter
50 g (1¾ oz) butter

### Jelly
2 gold-strength gelatine leaves or
   1 teaspoon powdered gelatine
¾ cup (180 ml/6 fl oz) chicken stock

Preheat the oven to 200°C (400°F/ Gas 6). Grease a six-hole ¾ cup (180 ml/6 fl oz) muffin tray.

To prepare the filling, cut 300 g (10½ oz) of the pork into 1 cm (³∕₈ in) cubes. Coarsely chop the remaining pork and place in a food processor. Add the bacon and blend to chop finely. Transfer to a bowl, add the diced pork, herbs and spices and season with salt and pepper. Set aside.

To make the pastry, sift the flour into a bowl and make a well in the centre. Pour in 1 egg and cover with a little flour. Put the lard, butter and 1 cup (250 ml/8½ fl oz) water in a small saucepan and heat over medium heat until the lard and butter have just melted and the water is hot. Pour into the well in the flour and, using a fork, mix until a dough begins to form. Turn out onto a clean work surface and knead to form a smooth dough. Shape into 2 discs and set aside to firm up slightly.

Roll the dough out between two sheets of baking paper, to 5 mm (¼ in) thick. Cut out six 14 cm (5½ in) circles and line the muffin holes. Cut out six more

10 cm (4 in) circles from the remaining pastry and set aside for the lids.

Spoon the filling into the pastry cases. Moisten the edge with water and place the lids on top. Pinch the edges together to seal. Brush the lids with egg and cut a 1 cm (³∕₈ in) circle out of the middle to create a hole.

Bake for 50 minutes, or until golden-brown. Set aside to cool, then refrigerate for at least 2 hours or until chilled.

To prepare the jelly, soak the gelatine leaves in a bowl of cold water for 5 minutes, or until softened. Heat the stock in a small saucepan. Squeeze the excess moisture out of the gelatine and add to the hot stock, stirring until melted. If using gelatine powder, dissolve in a little cold water and stir into the hot stock. Strain into a small jug. Using a funnel, slowly pour the jelly mixture through the holes in the lids, to fill the pies. Refrigerate overnight, or until the jelly is set. Serve cold with English mustard and cornichons.

# CORNISH PASTIES

MAKES 6

300 g (10½ oz) beef skirt steak,
   cut into 1 cm (³⁄₈ in) cubes
1 onion, cut into 1 cm (³⁄₈ in) dice
1 swede (rutabaga), cut into 1 cm
   (³⁄₈ in) dice
1 potato, cut into 1 cm (³⁄₈ in) dice
sea salt and freshly ground black pepper
1 large egg, lightly beaten, for glazing

PASTRY

75 g (2½ oz) lard, shortening or butter,
   diced and chilled in the freezer
75 g (2½ oz) butter, diced and chilled
   in the freezer
2 cups (300 g/10½ oz) plain
   (all-purpose) flour

To make the pastry, combine the lard, butter and flour in a food processor and pulse, until the mixture resembles fine crumbs. Gradually add ⅓ cup (80 ml/3 fl oz) chilled water, pulsing to incorporate, to form a dough. Turn out onto a clean work surface, gently knead and shape into a disc. Do not overwork. Wrap in plastic wrap and refrigerate for 30 minutes.

Preheat the oven to 200°C (400°F/Gas 6). Lightly grease a large baking tray.

Cut the pastry into 6 equal portions and roll out, one at a time, between two sheets of baking paper, to approximately 3 mm (⅛ in) thick. Cut an 18 cm (7 in) circle out of each pastry disc, approximately the size of a bread and butter plate.

Combine the beef, onion, swede and potato in a medium-sized bowl and season with salt and pepper. Spoon the filling, dividing it evenly, into the centre of the discs. Moisten the edge with water and bring together to meet in the middle to enclose the filling. Pinch with your fingers to seal.

Place the pasties on the prepared tray, the crimped edges facing up. Prick the pastry with a fork, to allow the steam to escape when cooking, and brush with egg. Bake for 40–45 minutes, or until they are golden-brown.

# ── Vegetable Pasties ──

1 cup finely diced onion
1 cup cubed swede (rutabaga)
1 cup cubed potato
1 cup cubed parsnip
1 celery stalk, diced
½ cup (60 g/2 oz) frozen peas
2 tablespoons chopped
   flat-leaf (Italian) parsley
2 garlic cloves, finely chopped
1 tablespoon finely chopped
   thyme
sea salt and freshly ground black pepper
1 large egg, lightly beaten, for glazing

### Pastry
150 g (5 oz) butter, diced and chilled
   in the freezer
2 cups (300 g/10½ oz) plain
   (all-purpose) flour

To make the pastry, combine the chilled butter with the flour in a food processor. Pulse until the mixture resembles fine crumbs. Gradually add ⅓ cup (80 ml/3 fl oz) chilled water, pulsing to incorporate, to form a dough. Turn out onto a clean work surface, gently knead and shape into a disc. Do not overwork. Wrap in plastic wrap and refrigerate for 30 minutes.

Preheat the oven to 200°C (400°F/ Gas 6). Lightly grease a large baking tray.

Cut the pastry into 6 equal portions and roll out, one at a time, between two sheets of baking paper, to approximately 3 mm (⅛ in) thick. Cut an 18 cm (7 in) circle out of each pastry disc, approximately the size of a bread and butter plate.

Combine the onion, swede, potato, parsnip, celery, peas, parsley, garlic and thyme in a medium-sized bowl and season with salt and pepper. Spoon the filling, dividing it evenly, into the centre of the discs. Moisten the edge with water and bring together to meet in the middle to enclose the filling. Pinch with your fingers to seal.

Place the pasties on the prepared baking tray with the crimped edges facing up. Prick the pastry with a fork, to allow the steam to escape when cooking, and brush with egg. Bake for 40–45 minutes, or until the pasties are golden-brown.

# PORK AND FENNEL SAUSAGE ROLLS

MAKES 8

1 tablespoon olive oil

1 brown onion, finely diced

2 garlic cloves, finely chopped

1 tablespoon fennel seeds, plus
   ½ teaspoon crushed, for sprinkling

½ carrot, coarsely grated

1 celery stalk, finely chopped

500 g (1 lb 2 oz) minced (ground) pork

½ granny smith apple, peeled and
   coarsely grated

1 teaspoon sea salt

½ teaspoon freshly ground black pepper

2 sheets frozen puff pastry, thawed

1 large egg, lightly beaten, for glazing

2 teaspoons sesame seeds, for sprinkling

Preheat the oven to 200°C (400°F/Gas 6). Line a large baking tray with baking paper.

Heat the oil in a large frying pan over low–medium heat. Cook the onion, garlic and fennel seeds until softened. Add the carrot and celery and cook for a further 10 minutes, or until softened. Transfer to a medium-sized bowl and set aside to cool.

Add the pork, apple, salt and pepper to the cooled vegetables and stir to combine. Shape the filling into 8 even-sized sausages.

Cut the puff pastry sheets into quarters and place the filling down the centre line of each pastry quarter. Brush one side of the pastry with egg and fold the pastry to enclose the filling. Turn the sausage rolls over and place them seam-side down on the prepared tray. Brush tops with egg and sprinkle with sesame and crushed fennel seeds.

Bake for 20–25 minutes, or until golden-brown and cooked through.

CLASSICS

Steak Diane

Steak with Sauces

Eggplant Parmigiana

Salt and Pepper
Calamari Salad

Nachos with
Chilli Beef

Bangers and Mash

Chicken Parmigiana

Fish and Chips

Beef Wellington

Chicken Kiev with
Garlic and
Porcini Butter

Coriander and Chilli-
crusted Lamb Cutlets
with Sweet Potato Mash

Veal Saltimbocca

Mushroom Risotto

Roast Chicken with
Thyme, Lemon and
Ricotta Stuffing

Roast Beef and
Yorkshire Puddings

Ploughman's Lunch

Maple and
Mustard-glazed Pork
Cutlets with Roasted
Apple Sauce

Ricotta and
Spinach Cannelloni

Fettuccine Carbonara

Pumpkin Gnocchi
with Sage Butter

Chicken Caesar Salad

# — Steak Diane —

4 × 200 g (7 oz) fillet steaks
1 tablespoon olive oil
sea salt and freshly ground black pepper
20 g (¾ oz) butter
4 French shallots, finely chopped
3 garlic cloves, finely chopped
3 tablespoons dijon mustard
3 tablespoons Worcestershire sauce
⅓ cup (80 ml/3 fl oz) brandy
1 cup (250 ml/8½ fl oz) pouring
  (whipping) cream
1 small handful flat-leaf (Italian) parsley,
  finely chopped

Preheat a large frying pan over high heat. Drizzle the steaks with oil and season with salt and pepper. Cook for 4 minutes on each side for medium or until cooked to your liking. Transfer to a plate, cover and set aside to rest while you prepare the sauce.

Reduce the heat to low–medium and melt the butter in the pan. Cook the shallot and garlic until softened. Add the mustard and Worcestershire sauce and stir to combine. Pour in the brandy and slightly tilt the pan to ignite the alcohol. Cook until it burns out. Add the cream and simmer for 1–2 minutes, until reduced slightly to make a sauce. Add the parsley and stir to combine.

Pour the sauce over the steaks to serve.

# — STEAK WITH SAUCES —

**SERVES 4**

### STEAK

**4 steaks, such as eye fillet, rib-eye, porterhouse or sirloin**
**olive oil, for brushing**
**salt and freshly ground black pepper**

Preheat a char-grill, flat grill or large frying pan over medium–high heat.

Brush the steaks with oil and season with salt and pepper. Grill for 3–4 minutes on each side for medium – timing may vary depending on size of steak – or until cooked to your liking. Transfer to a tray, cover and set aside in a warm place to rest for 5 minutes.

### GARLIC BUTTER
☞ **PREPARE IN ADVANCE**

**100 g (3½ oz) butter, at room temperature**
**2 garlic cloves, crushed**

Beat the butter and garlic together in a small bowl. Shape into a 6 cm (2¼ in) log and wrap in plastic wrap, twisting and tying the ends to secure. Refrigerate for 1 hour or until firm. Slice the log into 4 rounds, rewrap in plastic and refrigerate until required.

Place a butter portion on top of each cooked steak to serve.

### CLASSIC GRAVY
☞ **PREPARE WHILE STEAK IS RESTING**

**20 g (¾ oz) butter**
**2 tablespoons plain (all-purpose) flour**
**½ cup (125 ml/4 fl oz) red wine**
**2 cups (500 ml/17 fl oz) beef stock**

Add the butter to the pan in which you cooked the steak and melt over low–medium heat. Add the flour and cook, stirring with a wooden spoon, for 20 seconds. Pour in the wine and the stock, stirring to prevent lumps, and bring to the boil. Reduce the heat and gently simmer for 5 minutes, or until thick enough to coat the back of the spoon. Strain.

Pour sauce over the cooked steaks to serve.

## Green Peppercorn Sauce

☞ Prepare while steak
   is resting

20 g (³/₄ oz) butter
2 French shallots, finely chopped
1 garlic clove, crushed
1 tablespoon brandy
2 tablespoons green peppercorns in brine,
   drained and rinsed
1 cup (250 ml/8¹/₂ fl oz)
   pouring (whipping) cream
sea salt

Add the butter to the pan in
which you cooked the steak and
melt over low–medium heat.
Cook the shallot and garlic until
softened. Add the brandy, tilt the
pan slightly and ignite to burn off
the alcohol. Add the peppercorns
and cream and gently simmer
for 2 minutes, or until thickened
slightly, to coat the back of a
spoon. Season with salt.

Pour the sauce over the cooked
steaks to serve.

## Mushroom Sauce

☞ Prepare while steak
   is resting

20 g (³/₄ oz) butter
150 g (5 oz) button mushrooms, sliced
1 garlic clove, crushed
4 sprigs thyme
3 tablespoons dry white wine
1 cup (250 g/9 oz) crème fraîche
sea salt and ground white pepper

Add the butter to the pan in
which you cooked the steak and
melt over low–medium heat.
Cook the mushrooms, garlic and
thyme until the mushrooms are
softened and golden-brown. Add
the wine and crème fraîche and
gently simmer for 2 minutes or
until thickened slightly to coat
the back of a spoon. Remove the
thyme sprigs and season with
salt and white pepper.

Pour the sauce over the cooked
steaks to serve.

## Béarnaise Sauce

☞ Prepare up to 1 hour in
   advance or while steak
   is resting

¹/₂ cup (125 ml/4 fl oz) white vinegar
1 French shallot, finely chopped
2 black peppercorns
3 large egg yolks
200 g (7 oz) butter, cut into cubes
1 tablespoon lemon juice
1¹/₂ tablespoons finely chopped
   tarragon

Combine the vinegar, shallot and
peppercorns in a small saucepan
and simmer over medium heat
until reduced to 2 tablespoons
of liquid. Strain and transfer to a
heatproof bowl, add the egg yolks
and whisk to combine. Set the
bowl over a saucepan of barely
simmering water and whisk until
the mixture thickens and doubles
in size. Gradually add the butter,
3–4 cubes at a time, whisking
continuously until incorporated.
Stir in the lemon juice and
tarragon. Do not overheat or the
sauce will split. If making the
sauce in advance, keep warm.

Pour the sauce over the cooked
steaks to serve.

# — Eggplant Parmigiana —

**Serves 8**

3 large eggplants (aubergines),
   sliced lengthways 1 cm (³⁄₈ in) thick
salt, for sprinkling
plain (all-purpose) flour, for coating
3 large eggs, lightly beaten
2 cups (120 g/4 oz) fresh breadcrumbs
¹⁄₃ cup (80 ml/3 fl oz) olive oil
¹⁄₃ cup (80 ml/3 fl oz) vegetable oil
400 g (14 oz) fresh mozzarella
   or bocconcini, sliced
1¹⁄₂ cups (120 g/4 oz)
   coarsely grated parmesan
12 basil leaves, torn

Passata (puréed tomatoes)
2 tablespoons olive oil
1 onion, finely chopped
2 garlic cloves, finely chopped
2 × 400 g (14 oz) tins chopped tomatoes
sea salt and freshly ground black pepper

Sprinkle both sides of the eggplant slices with salt. Arrange on wire racks and set aside for 1 hour.

Make the passata (puréed tomatoes). Heat the oil in a medium saucepan over low–medium heat. Cook the onion and garlic, until softened; add the tomato and cook for 5 minutes, or until thickened slightly. Season with salt and pepper.

Preheat the oven to 180°C (350°F/Gas 4).

Rinse the eggplant slices and pat dry using paper towel. Put the flour, eggs and breadcrumbs into separate bowls. Coat the eggplant in flour, followed by egg and lastly breadcrumbs, pressing gently to secure.

Heat the olive and vegetable oils together in a large frying pan over medium–high heat. Fry the eggplant slices, a few at a time, for 1 minute on each side or until golden-brown. Transfer to paper towel to drain.

Spread a little of the passata over the base of a deep 33 cm × 23 cm (13 in × 9 in) ovenproof dish. Arrange a layer of eggplant over the top and scatter with a third of the mozzarella, parmesan and basil. Spread a third of the remaining passata over the top. Repeat, to create another three layers.

Cover with foil and bake in the oven for 30 minutes. Uncover and bake for a further 15–20 minutes, or until golden-brown. Cut into portions to serve.

# SALT AND PEPPER CALAMARI SALAD

### SALT AND PEPPER CALAMARI
**600 g (1 lb 5 oz) calamari tubes**
**juice of 1 lemon**
**1½ tablespoons sea salt**
**2 teaspoons Sichuan peppercorns**
**½ teaspoon dried chilli flakes**
**½ cup (75 g/2½ oz) cornflour (cornstarch)**
**vegetable oil, for deep-frying**

### SALAD
**250 g (9 oz) snow peas**
  **(mangetout), trimmed**
**2 large handfuls mixed watercress,**
  **mizuna and tatsoi**
**1 Lebanese (short) cucumber,**
  **halved lengthways and thinly sliced**
**2 spring onions (scallions), cut into 5 cm**
  **(2 in) lengths and thinly sliced into strips**
**1 large handful coriander (cilantro)**
**2 tablespoons rice wine vinegar**
**1 garlic clove, crushed**
**½ teaspoon sugar**
**3 tablespoons olive oil**
**2 teaspoons sesame oil**

To prepare the calamari, cut lengthways down one side of the tubes and open out flat. Rinse under cold water. Score the inside of the tubes, making a pattern of shallow diagonal cuts across the length of the tube. Cut the tubes in half crossways and then into 3 cm (1¼ in) wide strips. Place in a medium-sized bowl, add the lemon juice and toss to coat. Cover and refrigerate for 30 minutes.

Grind the sea salt, Sichuan peppercorns and chilli flakes together using a mortar and pestle. Transfer to a small bowl and set aside.

To prepare the salad, bring a medium saucepan of water to the boil over high heat. Blanch the snow peas, drain and refresh in iced water. Drain.

Combine the snow peas, mixed leaves, cucumber, spring onion and coriander in a large bowl.

Combine the vinegar, garlic and sugar together in a small bowl. Gradually whisk in the olive and sesame oils. Set aside.

Two-thirds fill a deep-fryer or a large heavy-based saucepan with vegetable oil and heat to 190°C (375°F).

Drain the calamari and pat dry with paper towel. Toss the calamari in cornflour and fry in batches, for 1 minute or until crisp and golden. Drain on paper towel. Season with the prepared salt and pepper mixture.

Add the dressing to the salad and toss to coat. Serve the salad topped with salt and pepper calamari.

# — Nachos with Chilli Beef —

**Serves 4**

230 g (8 oz) packet plain corn chips
2 cups (250 g/9 oz) grated tasty cheese
1 cup (250 g/9 oz) sour cream

### Chilli Beef

2 tablespoons olive oil
1 small brown onion, finely chopped
1 garlic clove, crushed
2 teaspoons ground cumin
1/2 teaspoon cayenne pepper
1/4 teaspoon ground cinnamon
1/2 teaspoon chilli powder
400 g (14 oz) minced (ground) beef
1/2 cup (125 ml/4 fl oz) beef stock
2 tomatoes, diced
1 tablespoon tomato paste
   (concentrated tomato purée)
1 tablespoon finely chopped oregano
1 jalapeño chilli, finely chopped
1 × 400 g (14 oz) tin kidney beans,
   drained and rinsed

### Tomato Salsa

3 ripe tomatoes, diced
1/2 red onion, diced
1 small handful coriander (cilantro)
1 jalapeño chilli, finely diced
1 tablespoon red wine vinegar
2 tablespoons olive oil
sea salt and freshly ground black pepper

### Guacamole

2 ripe avocados, halved lengthways
   and stones removed
juice of 1 lime
1 garlic clove, crushed
1–3 dashes Tabasco sauce, to taste
sea salt and freshly ground black pepper

To make the chilli beef, heat the oil in a medium heavy-based saucepan and cook the onion and garlic until softened. Add the spices and cook for 20 seconds, or until fragrant. Increase the heat to medium, add the beef and cook, breaking up the lumps, for 10 minutes or until browned. Add the stock, tomato, tomato paste, oregano and jalapeño and bring to the boil. Cover and simmer for 30–40 minutes, or until tender. Add the beans and cook uncovered for a further 10 minutes, or until the sauce is thick.

Meanwhile to make the tomato salsa, combine all the ingredients in a medium-sized bowl, seasoning to taste with salt and pepper.

To make the guacamole, scoop the avocado flesh into a medium-sized bowl, add the lime juice and garlic and mash using a potato masher. Add Tabasco sauce to taste and season with salt and pepper.

Preheat the oven to 180°C (350°F/Gas 4).

Divide half of the corn chips among four large ovenproof serving bowls or plates and sprinkle with half of the cheese. Cover with the remaining chips, spoon on the chilli beef and sprinkle with the remaining cheese. Bake in the oven for 15 minutes, or until the cheese has melted.

Serve topped with salsa, a dollop of guacamole and sour cream.

# — BANGERS AND MASH —

2 tablespoons olive oil
Creamy Roast Garlic Potato Mash
  (page 119)

SKINLESS PORK AND HERB SAUSAGES
750 g (1 lb 10 oz) minced (ground) pork
3 tablespoons red wine
2 garlic cloves, crushed
2 tablespoons finely chopped oregano
1 tablespoon finely chopped thyme
1 tablespoon olive oil
2 teaspoons sea salt
1 teaspoon freshly ground black pepper
1 teaspoon fennel seeds, crushed
1 teaspoon chilli flakes, crushed

ONION GRAVY
1 tablespoon olive oil
20 g (¾ oz) butter
2 brown onions, thinly sliced
2 tablespoons plain (all-purpose) flour
½ cup (125 ml/4 fl oz) red wine
1 cup (250 ml/8½ fl oz) beef stock

To make the sausages, place all the ingredients in a medium-sized bowl and using clean hands, mix and knead together until sticky and combined well. Shape the mixture into 8 even-sized sausages, put on a plate and cover and refrigerate for at least 1 hour or overnight.

To prepare the onion gravy, heat the oil and butter together in a large frying pan over low–medium heat. Cook the onion until softened and golden. Transfer to a plate. Add the flour to the pan and cook, stirring with a wooden spoon, for 20 seconds. Pour in the wine and the stock, stirring to prevent lumps, and bring to the boil. Reduce the heat and gently simmer for 5 minutes, or until thick enough to coat the back of the spoon. Return the onion to the pan and stir to combine. Keep warm until required.

Heat the oil in a large frying pan over medium heat and cook the sausages for 10 minutes, turning occasionally, until brown all over.

Serve the sausages with potato mash and onion gravy.

# — CHICKEN PARMIGIANA —

4 skinless chicken breast fillets
⅓ cup (50 g/1¾ oz)
   plain (all-purpose) flour
2 large eggs, lightly beaten
vegetable oil, for shallow-frying
4 slices smoked ham
4 slices mozzarella

### PARMESAN AND HERB CRUMBS
1 loaf day-old, unsliced white bread, crust
   removed and bread roughly chopped
½ cup (50 g/1¾ oz) finely grated parmesan
2 tablespoons chopped oregano

### NAPOLI SAUCE
1 kg (2 lb 3 oz) vine-ripened tomatoes
2 tablespoons olive oil
1 small brown onion, finely chopped
2 garlic cloves, finely chopped
1 tablespoon tomato paste
   (concentrated tomato purée)
1 teaspoon sugar
2 tablespoons finely chopped oregano
1 small handful basil, chopped
salt and freshly ground black pepper

Preheat the oven to 120°C (250°F/ Gas ¼–½).

To prepare the crumbs, spread the bread on a baking tray. Bake for 15–20 minutes, turning occasionally, to dry out slightly; the bread should not be completely dry, just with a stale texture. Blend in batches in a food processor, until coarse. Transfer 2 cups of the crumbs to a large bowl. Stir in the parmesan and oregano and set aside. Store leftover crumbs in an airtight container in the refrigerator for up to 1 week.

To make the napoli sauce, bring a saucepan of water to the boil. Score a cross in the base of the tomatoes and remove the cores. Blanch the tomatoes for 10 seconds, or until the skins begin to lift from the flesh. Drain and refresh under cold water. Peel the tomatoes and discard the skins. Cut in half and remove and discard the seeds. Coarsely chop the flesh. Heat the oil in a heavy-based saucepan and cook the onion and garlic until softened. Add the tomato and cook, stirring occasionally, for 10 minutes or

until the tomato softens. Add the tomato paste, sugar and oregano and gently simmer for 10–15 minutes, to make a thick sauce. Stir in the basil and season with salt and pepper.

Increase the oven temperature to 180°C (350°F/Gas 4).

Butterfly the thickest part of the chicken. Place between two sheets of baking paper and using a meat mallet, flatten the chicken breasts out to an even thickness. Coat the chicken in flour, dip in egg then coat in parmesan and herb crumbs, pressing gently to secure.

Heat enough oil to shallow-fry, about 2 cm (¾ in), in a large frying pan over medium heat. Cook the chicken for 2–3 minutes on each side, or until golden-brown and just cooked. Drain on paper towel.

Arrange the crumbed chicken on two baking trays. Spoon napoli on top and cover with a slice each of smoked ham and mozzarella. Bake in the oven for 10 minutes or until the cheese has melted.

# Fish and Chips

SERVES 4

1½ cups (225 g/8 oz) plain (all-purpose) flour, plus extra for coating
1 teaspoon baking powder
1½ cups (375 ml/12½ fl oz) chilled beer (such as lager)
800 g (1 lb 12 oz) flathead tails or other firm white fish fillets
vegetable oil, for deep-frying
sea salt
Twice-cooked Chips (page 118)
lemon wedges, to serve

Tartare Sauce
2 large egg yolks
1 teaspoon dijon mustard
1 tablespoon lemon juice
1 cup (250 ml/8½ fl oz) light olive oil
2 tablespoons finely chopped cornichons
2 tablespoons finely chopped red onion
2 tablespoons capers, rinsed and finely chopped
2 tablespoons finely chopped chives
1 tablespoon finely chopped flat-leaf (Italian) parsley

Sift the flour and baking powder together into a medium-sized bowl. Gradually add the beer, whisking until smooth. Cover the batter and refrigerate for 30 minutes.

To make the tartare sauce, whisk the egg yolks, mustard and lemon juice together in a small bowl. Gradually pour in the oil, whisking continuously, until thick. Add the remaining ingredients and stir to combine. Set aside.

Two-thirds fill a deep-fryer or a large heavy-based saucepan with vegetable oil and heat to 190°C (375°F).

Toss the fish in flour and dredge in batter. Cook in batches for 3–4 minutes, or until crisp and golden-brown. Transfer to paper towel, to drain.

Season the fish and serve with twice-cooked chips, tartare sauce and lemon wedges.

# BEEF WELLINGTON

4 × 200 g (7 oz) fillet steaks
1 tablespoon olive oil
sea salt and freshly ground black pepper
20 g (¾ oz) butter
1 onion, finely chopped
1 garlic clove, finely chopped
250 g (9 oz) button mushrooms,
   finely chopped
3 sprigs thyme
100 g (3½ oz) chicken liver pâté
4 sheets frozen puff pastry, thawed
1 large egg, lightly beaten

Preheat the oven to 200°C (400°F/Gas 6).

Preheat a large frying pan over high heat. Drizzle the steaks with oil, season with salt and pepper, then sear for 3–4 minutes or until browned all over. Transfer to a tray and set aside to cool. Refrigerate until cold.

Reduce the heat to low and add the butter to the pan. Cook the onion and garlic, until softened. Add the mushroom and thyme and cook until softened and the liquid has evaporated. Transfer to a small bowl, discard the thyme sprigs and set aside to cool slightly. Refrigerate until cold.

Spread the pâté on top of the cooled steaks and top with mushroom mixture. Cover each steak with a pastry sheet, fold the corners underneath and trim off any excess pastry. Cut leaves out of the excess pastry and arrange on top of the beef parcels, to decorate. Transfer to a baking tray and brush with egg.

Bake for 20 minutes, or until puffed and golden-brown.

# — Chicken Kiev with —
# — Garlic and Porcini Butter —

5 g (¼ oz) dried porcini mushrooms
120 g (4 oz) unsalted butter, softened
2 garlic cloves, finely chopped
2 tablespoons finely chopped
  flat-leaf (Italian) parsley
4 large skinless chicken breast fillets
2 large eggs
2 tablespoons milk
3 tablespoons plain (all-purpose) flour
3 cups (240 g/9 oz) fresh breadcrumbs
vegetable oil, for deep-frying

Soak the porcini mushrooms in 3 tablespoons warm water for 30 minutes. Strain and finely chop.

Put the butter, garlic, porcini and parsley in a small bowl and mix well to combine. Divide into 4 equal portions and shape into 6 cm (2¼ in) long logs. Refrigerate for 15 minutes or until firm.

Butterfly the thickest part of the chicken. Place the chicken breasts between two sheets of baking paper and using a meat mallet, flatten out to approximately 5 mm (¼ in) thick, taking care not to tear any holes, as this will cause the butter to leak.

Place a butter log across each chicken breast at the widest end. Fold the sides in, then the end over to cover the butter. Roll up to completely enclose.

Lightly beat the eggs with the milk. Double crumb the chicken parcels, coating in flour, then egg and breadcrumbs and then just egg and breadcrumbs for the second coat, pressing gently to secure. Place on a tray, cover and refrigerate for 1 hour.

Preheat the oven to 180°C (350°F/Gas 4). Two-thirds fill a deep-fryer or a large, deep, heavy-based saucepan with vegetable oil and heat to 190°C (375°F). Place a clean wire rack on a baking tray, for draining.

Deep-fry the chicken parcels two at a time, for 5 minutes or until golden. Transfer to the wire rack and bake for 10 minutes, to complete cooking.

# Coriander and Chilli-crusted Lamb Cutlets with Sweet Potato Mash

**SERVES 4**

1 large handful coriander (cilantro), chopped
1 tablespoon olive oil
2 long red chillies, deseeded and finely chopped
1 small red chilli, deseeded and finely chopped
2 garlic cloves, finely chopped
finely grated zest of 1 orange
sea salt and freshly ground black pepper
12 lamb cutlets

**Sweet Potato Mash**
2 sweet potatoes, quartered
40 g (1½ oz) butter, softened

Combine the coriander, oil, chillies, garlic and orange zest in a medium-sized bowl, season with salt and pepper and set aside.

Put the sweet potato in a saucepan, cover with cold salted water and bring to the boil over high heat. Cook for 10 minutes, or until tender. Drain and return to the pan. Add the butter and mash using a potato masher. Keep warm.

Preheat a large frying pan on medium–high heat.

Coat the lamb cutlets in the coriander and chilli mixture and cook for 2 minutes on each side for medium–rare, or until cooked to your liking. Serve with sweet potato mash.

# Veal Saltimbocca

**4 × 150 g (5 oz) veal loin steaks**
**sea salt and freshly ground black pepper**
**8 sage leaves**
**8 slices prosciutto**
**olive oil, for drizzling**

Place the veal steaks between two sheets of baking paper and using a meat mallet flatten out to approximately 5 mm (¼ in) thick.

Season the veal with salt and pepper. Place two sage leaves on each steak, cover with two slices of prosciutto and wrap them around, tucking the ends underneath.

Preheat a large frying pan over medium–high heat. Drizzle the wrapped veal with oil and cook, sage-side down first, for 2 minutes on each side or until the prosciutto is crisp and golden-brown and the veal is cooked through.

# — Mushroom Risotto —

20 g (³/₄ oz) dried porcini mushrooms
3 cups (750 ml/25 fl oz) chicken stock
80 g (3 oz) butter
500 g (1 lb 2 oz) mixed mushrooms,
  such as Swiss brown and button,
  thickly sliced
2 tablespoons chopped oregano
2 tablespoons olive oil
1 onion, finely diced
2 garlic cloves, finely chopped
1½ cups (300 g/10½ oz) risotto rice
125 ml (½ cup/4 fl oz) dry white wine
½ cup (50 g/1¾ oz)
  freshly grated parmesan
sea salt and freshly ground black pepper
shaved parmesan, to serve

Soak the porcini mushrooms in 1 cup (250 ml/8½ fl oz) warm water for 30 minutes. Strain, reserving the liquid. Finely slice the mushrooms and set aside.

Combine the reserved mushroom liquid and the stock in a saucepan and bring to a simmer. Reduce the heat to low and keep warm.

Melt half of the butter in a wide heavy-based saucepan over medium heat. Add the mixed mushrooms and oregano and cook until softened and golden-brown. Transfer to a bowl and set aside.

Add the oil to the pan and heat over medium. Cook the onion, garlic and porcini mushrooms until softened. Add the rice, stir to coat and cook for 1 minute, or until just toasted. Pour in the wine and stir until it has been almost completely absorbed. Add the stock ⅓ cup (80 ml/3 fl oz) at a time, stirring continuously, ensuring it is completely absorbed before adding additional stock. Continue in this manner until all of the stock has been absorbed and the rice is cooked *al dente*, approximately 20–25 minutes.

Add the cooked mushrooms, grated parmesan and remaining butter and stir to combine. Season with salt and pepper.

Serve topped with shaved parmesan and additional ground pepper, if desired.

☞ If porcini mushrooms are unavailable, omit and increase the stock measure to 4 cups (1 litre/34 fl oz).

# Roast Chicken with Thyme, Lemon and Ricotta Stuffing

200 g (7 oz) fresh ricotta
1 tablespoon thyme
finely grated zest of 2 lemons
¼ teaspoon dried chilli flakes, crushed
sea salt and freshly ground black pepper
4 chicken marylands (chicken leg
  quarters)
600 g (1 lb 5 oz) kipfler (fingerling)
  potatoes
4 large red onions, cut in half crossways
olive oil, for drizzling

Preheat the oven to 200°C (400°F/Gas 6).

Combine the ricotta, thyme, lemon zest and chilli flakes in a small bowl. Season with salt and pepper. Divide the mixture into 4 equal portions and stuff under the skin of the marylands.

Arrange the stuffed marylands in a baking tray with the potatoes and onion halves around the chicken. Drizzle with oil and season with salt and pepper.

Roast, turning the potatoes and onions occasionally, for 30–35 minutes, or until the chicken is golden-brown and cooked through and the potatoes and onion are tender.

# Roast Beef and Yorkshire Puddings

**Serves 4**

3 all-purpose potatoes, quartered
1 kg (2 lb 3 oz) whole scotch fillet
olive oil, for drizzling
2 tablespoons seeded mustard
1 tablespoon chopped thyme
1 tablespoon chopped rosemary
sea salt and freshly ground black pepper
¼ pumpkin (winter squash),  cut into
   5 cm (2 in) chunks
4 small brown onions

### Yorkshire Puddings
¾ cup (120 g/4 oz) plain (all-purpose) flour
½ teaspoon sea salt
1 cup (250 ml/8½ fl oz) milk
1 large egg
3 tablespoons lard, vegetable oil or
   melted butter

### Gravy
2 tablespoons plain (all-purpose) flour
½ cup (125 ml/4 fl oz) red wine
1 cup (250 ml/8½ fl oz) beef stock

Preheat the oven to 220°C (430°F/Gas 7). Place a wire rack in the base of a large baking tray.

Put the potatoes in a saucepan, cover with cold water and bring to the boil. Cook for 5 minutes. Drain.

Cover the beef with oil, mustard, herbs, and salt and pepper, and place on the rack. Put the potatoes, pumpkin and onions around the beef and drizzle with oil. Cook for 15 minutes.

For the yorkshire pudding batter, sift the flour and salt together in a bowl and make a well in the centre. Lightly beat the milk and egg together and pour into the well. Whisk to a smooth batter and set aside.

Reduce the oven temperature to 180°C (350°F/Gas 4). Cook beef for 25 minutes, for medium, or until cooked to your liking. Transfer the beef and vegetables onto a tray, cover with foil and keep warm. Set the baking tray aside for gravy.

Increase the oven temperature to 240°C (460°F/Gas 8–9).

Divide the lard or vegetable oil among four holes of a ¾ cup (180 ml/6 fl oz) capacity muffin tray and heat in the oven for 5 minutes or until almost smoking. Carefully remove the tray from the oven. Quickly pour the Yorkshire pudding batter into the prepared muffin holes. Cook for 15 minutes, or until puffed and golden-brown.

To make the gravy, place the baking tray over medium heat, add the flour to the meat fat and juices and cook, stirring constantly, for 30 seconds, or until it begins to colour. Pour in the wine and stock and simmer, stirring occasionally and scraping cooked particles from the base of the tray with a wooden spoon, until the gravy thickens. Add any juices from the rested meat. Strain through a fine-mesh sieve into a gravy boat or heatproof jug which has been preheated with boiling water.

Carve the beef into thick slices and serve with roast vegetables, Yorkshire puddings and gravy.

# — Ploughman's Lunch —

1 crusty country-style baguette
  or 4 crusty bread rolls, thickly sliced
250 g (9 oz) stilton
400 g (14 oz) English cheddar
1 crisp red apple, quartered
1 crisp pear, quartered
8 pickled onions, homemade
  (see recipe below) or store bought
½ cup (125 ml/4 fl oz) Branston or other
  sweet brown pickle
½ cup (125 ml/4 fl oz) piccalilli or other
  spiced mustard relish

Pickled Onions
1 kg (2 lb 3 oz) pickling onions
3 tablespoons salt
4 cups (1 litre/34 fl oz) white vinegar
½ cup (110 g/3¾ oz) sugar
4 bay leaves
2 teaspoons black peppercorns
2 teaspoons allspice berries
3 whole cloves
4 small dried chillies (optional),
  for an added kick

To prepare your own pickled onions, peel the onions and place them in a large container or bucket. Combine the salt with 4 cups (1 litre/34 fl oz) water in a large bowl, stirring until the salt dissolves. Pour over the onions, cover with baking paper and weigh down, if necessary, to keep them submerged. Cover and set aside at room temperature for 24 hours.

Combine the vinegar, sugar, bay leaves, peppercorns, allspice berries, cloves and chillies, if desired, in a saucepan and gently simmer over low–medium heat, stirring occasionally, until the sugar dissolves. Set aside to cool completely.

Drain the onions and rinse under cold running water.

Pack the onions into four 3 cup (750 ml/25 fl oz) capacity sterilised jars. Pour the cooled vinegar pickling liquid over the top to cover. Seal the jars and leave for 3 weeks to pickle before using.

To assemble the ploughman's lunch, arrange the bread, cheeses, fruit and pickled onions on a large platter. Put the pickle and relish in two small dishes and set on the platter. Serve with butter knives.

# Maple and Mustard-glazed Pork Cutlets with Roasted Apple Sauce

**SERVES 4**

4 × 200 g (7 oz) pork cutlets
2 tablespoons maple syrup
2 tablespoons seeded mustard
1 tablespoon cider vinegar
1 garlic clove, crushed
sea salt and freshly ground black pepper

ROASTED APPLE SAUCE
3 granny smith apples
20 g (¾ oz) butter
1 tablespoon cider vinegar
2 teaspoons caster (superfine) sugar

Preheat the oven to 200°C (400°F/Gas 6).

Core the apples, using an apple corer, place the apples on a baking tray and roast in the oven for 25–30 minutes, or until tender. Set aside to cool slightly.

Combine the maple syrup, mustard, vinegar and garlic in a small bowl. Season with salt and pepper.

Preheat a char-grill plate or large frying pan over medium–high heat.

Brush the pork cutlets with the maple and mustard glaze and cook for 3–4 minutes on each side, or until just cooked through. Transfer to a tray, cover and set aside for 5 minutes to rest.

When cool enough to handle, peel the skin off the apples and coarsely chop the flesh. Melt the butter in a saucepan over low–medium heat. Add the apple, vinegar and sugar and cook, stirring occasionally, until reduced to make a thick sauce.

Serve the pork cutlets with apple sauce.

# Ricotta and Spinach Cannelloni

**Serves 6**

3 tablespoons olive oil

1 onion, finely chopped

2 garlic cloves, finely chopped

300 g (10 oz) spinach leaves
   (approximately 1 bunch), finely shredded

600 g (1 lb 5 oz) fresh ricotta

1 cup (100 g/3½ oz) coarsely grated
   parmesan

½ teaspoon ground nutmeg

finely grated zest of 1 lemon

sea salt and freshly ground black pepper

12 fresh cannelloni sheets

2 balls buffalo mozzarella

Tomato Ketchup

2 tablespoons olive oil

1 small onion, finely chopped

2 garlic cloves, finely chopped

3 cups (750 ml/25 fl oz)
   passata (puréed tomatoes)

sea salt and freshly ground black pepper

Preheat the oven to 180°C (350°F/Gas 4). Lightly grease a 4 cm (1½ in) deep, 30 cm × 20 cm (12 in × 8 in) ovenproof baking dish.

Heat the oil in a large saucepan over low–medium heat and cook the onion and garlic, until softened. Add the spinach and cook, until wilted. Strain in a colander, using the back of a spoon to push out excess liquid.

Combine the spinach mixture, ricotta, 80 g (3 oz) of the parmesan, the nutmeg and lemon zest in a medium-sized bowl. Season with salt and pepper and set aside.

Prepare the cannelloni sheets as per packet instructions. Lay the sheets out on a clean work surface. Spread 3 tablespoons of filling down the length of one edge of the sheets and roll up to enclose the filling. Arrange the filled tubes in a single layer in the prepared dish.

To make the tomato ketchup, heat the oil in a small saucepan over low–medium heat and cook the onion and garlic, until softened. Add the passata and stir to combine. Season with salt and pepper.

Pour the sauce over the cannelloni. Tear the mozzarella balls into pieces and scatter over the top. Sprinkle with the remaining parmesan. Bake for 30 minutes or until golden-brown and the pasta is tender. Cut into portions to serve.

# Fettuccine Carbonara

500 g (1 lb 2 oz) dried fettuccine
1 tablespoon olive oil
150 g (5 oz) slices prosciutto
½ cup (125 ml/4 fl oz)
　pouring (whipping) cream
60 g (2 oz) shaved parmesan, plus extra
　to serve
4 large eggs, lightly beaten
salt and freshly ground black pepper

Cook the pasta in a large saucepan of boiling salted water for 8–10 minutes, or until *al dente*.

Meanwhile, heat the oil in a large frying pan. Cook the prosciutto, until crisp. Remove from the heat.

Drain the pasta, reserving approximately 2 tablespoons of the cooking liquid.

Return the frying pan with the prosciutto to the heat. Pour in the cream and bring to a gentle simmer. Add the parmesan and stir to combine. Add the pasta and reserved liquid and toss to coat. Add the eggs, and toss to combine and just cooked. Be careful not to overcook or they will scramble. Remove from the heat and season with salt.

Serve immediately, topped with extra shaved parmesan and pepper.

# Pumpkin Gnocchi with Sage Butter

**Serves 4**

600 g (1 lb 5 oz) butternut pumpkin
  (squash), quartered and seeded,
  skin left on
400 g (14 oz) all-purpose potatoes,
  such as desiree or nicola, unpeeled
1 cup (150 g/5 oz) plain (all-purpose) flour,
  plus extra for dusting
sea salt and ground white pepper
shaved parmesan, to serve

**Browned Sage Butter**
150 g (5 oz) butter
1 small handful sage

Preheat the oven to 180°C (350°F/ Gas 4).

Put the pumpkin on a baking tray and roast in the oven for 45 minutes, or until tender but not browned.

Meanwhile steam the potatoes, whole and unpeeled, for 20–25 minutes or until tender when tested with a skewer. Peel the potatoes while still hot and mash. Press the mash through a sieve or fine strainer into a large bowl, using the back of a spoon to push it through.

Line a baking tray with clean paper towel and lightly dust with some extra flour.

Scrape the pumpkin flesh off the skin, add to the potato and stir to combine. Add the flour and mix until just combined. Season with salt and white pepper. Turn out onto a clean, lightly floured work surface. Divide into quarters and roll into lengths 2 cm (¾ in) thick. Cut into 3 cm (1¼ in) pieces and place on the prepared tray.

Bring a large saucepan of salted water to the boil. Cook the gnocchi in batches for 3–4 minutes or until they float to the surface. Remove using a slotted spoon and set aside on a tray, while you cook the remaining gnocchi.

To make the sage butter, preheat a large frying pan over medium heat. Add the butter and cook for 3–5 minutes, until it foams and turns nut-brown. Add the sage and swirl to coat.

Drain the gnocchi of excess water and add to the sage butter. Toss to coat. Serve topped with shaved parmesan.

# Chicken Caesar Salad

**SERVES 4**

80 g (3 oz) butter

2 garlic cloves, crushed

3 slices sourdough bread,
   cut into 2 cm (³/₄ in) cubes

8 slices prosciutto

2 skinless chicken breast fillets

olive oil

sea salt and freshly ground black pepper

3 baby cos (romaine) lettuces,
   leaves separated

2 tablespoons white vinegar

4 large eggs

¹/₂ cup (40 g/1¹/₂ oz) shaved parmesan,
   plus extra to serve

4 anchovy fillets, cut into thin strips

### Anchovy Dressing

2 large egg yolks

2 tablespoons white wine vinegar

1 tablespoon finely grated parmesan

2 teaspoons Worcestershire sauce

3 anchovy fillets

1 teaspoon dijon mustard

1 garlic clove, coarsely chopped

1 cup (250 ml/8¹/₂ fl oz) olive oil

sea salt and ground white pepper

Preheat the oven to 180°C (350°F/ Gas 4).

Melt the butter in a small saucepan. Pour into a small bowl, leaving the white sediment behind in the pan. Add the garlic and stir to combine. Place the cubed bread in a baking tray, drizzle with the garlic butter and toss to coat. Bake, tossing occasionally, for 10 minutes or until golden-brown. Drain on paper towel.

Lay the prosciutto on a baking tray and cook for 5–10 minutes, until crisp and golden-brown. Break into smaller pieces and transfer to paper towel, to drain.

To make the dressing, place all the ingredients except the oil and salt and pepper in a small food processor and blend until smooth. Gradually add the oil in a thin, steady stream, blending until thick and creamy. Transfer to a small bowl and season with salt and white pepper.

Preheat a char-grill plate or large frying pan over medium–high heat. Drizzle the chicken with oil and season with salt and pepper. Grill for 4–5 minutes on each side, or until golden-brown and cooked through. Transfer to a plate, cover and set aside for 5 minutes, to rest. Roughly tear the large outer cos leaves, trim the small inner leaves and combine in a large bowl. Cut the chicken into bite-sized pieces. Add the chicken and parmesan to the salad.

Bring a saucepan of water to a gentle simmer. Add the vinegar and using a spoon, create a whirlpool in the water. Crack the eggs, one at a time, into the whirlpool. Cook for 2 minutes for a soft centre, or until poached to your liking. Using a slotted spoon, remove the eggs, straining off excess water, and transfer to paper towel, to drain.

Pour enough dressing over the salad to coat and toss to combine. Arrange the salad on serving plates. Sprinkle with prosciutto, croutons and extra parmesan. Top with poached egg, anchovies and freshly ground black pepper. Serve immediately.

Buttermilk Fried Chicken with Chipotle Mayonnaise

Chinese Barbecue Pork Spare Ribs

Gremolata-crumbed Veal Schnitzel

Prawn and Chorizo Paella

Mussels with Tomato and Chilli

Soft Polenta with Mushrooms and Pesto

Rabbit Cacciatore

Thai Beef and Noodle Salad

Slow-cooked Five-spice Pork Belly with Chinese Broccoli

Moroccan Spiced Lamb Shanks with Date and Roasted Almond Couscous

Chicken Tikka Masala

Osso Bucco

Kingfish Niçoise Salad

# Buttermilk Fried Chicken with Chipotle Mayonnaise

2 cups (500 ml/17 fl oz) buttermilk
½ onion, coarsely grated
2 teaspoons dried oregano
1 teaspoon mild sweet paprika
1 garlic clove, crushed
1.5 kg (3 lb 5 oz) chicken thigh and
   drumstick pieces, skin on
vegetable oil, for deep-frying
lime wedges, to serve

### Spice Coating
2 cups (300 g/10½ oz)
   plain (all-purpose) flour
1 tablespoon mild sweet paprika
2 teaspoons onion powder
2 teaspoons garlic powder
2 teaspoons salt
½ teaspoon cayenne pepper

### Chipotle Mayonnaise
3 large egg yolks
1 teaspoon dijon mustard
1 tablespoon lime juice
1½ cups (375 ml/12½ fl oz) light olive oil
1 chipotle chilli in 2 teaspoons
   adobo sauce, puréed
sea salt

Combine the buttermilk, onion, oregano, paprika and garlic in a medium-sized bowl. Add the chicken pieces, cover with plastic wrap and refrigerate overnight.

Remove the chicken from the buttermilk and drain in a colander. Strain the buttermilk into a medium-sized bowl, discarding the solids.

Combine the spice-coating ingredients in a large zip-lock bag. Add the chicken pieces, a few at a time, and shake to coat. Dip the chicken in the reserved buttermilk and coat again in the spiced flour. Arrange on a wire rack and set aside for 15 minutes, to dry slightly.

Meanwhile make the mayonnaise: whisk the egg yolks, mustard and lime juice together in a small bowl. Gradually pour in the oil, whisking continuously, until thick. Add the chipotle and adobo purée and stir to combine. Season with salt. Transfer to a small serving bowl, cover and refrigerate.

Two-thirds fill a deep-fryer or a large heavy-based saucepan with vegetable oil and heat to 190°C (375°F). Place a clean wire rack on a baking tray, for draining. Cook the chicken in batches for 8–10 minutes, until crisp, golden-brown and the juices run clear when a skewer is inserted into the thickest part of the flesh. Drain on the rack.

Serve hot with chipotle mayonnaise and lime wedges.

☞ This recipe needs to be prepared 1 day in advance.

# CHINESE BARBECUE
# PORK SPARE RIBS

1.5 kg (3 lb 5 oz) Chinese-style pork
spare ribs, cut crossways into 5 cm
(2 in) lengths (ask your butcher to do
this for you)
steamed rice, to serve
2 spring onions (scallions), cut into 8 cm
(3¼ in) lengths and thinly sliced into
strips, to garnish

BARBECUE MARINADE
½ cup (125 ml/4 fl oz) hoisin sauce
3 tablespoons light soy sauce
3 tablespoons Shaoxing (Chinese)
rice wine
3 tablespoons tomato ketchup
2 tablespoons honey
4 garlic cloves, crushed
3 cm (1¼ in) piece ginger, peeled and
finely grated

To make the marinade, combine all of the ingredients in a small saucepan and bring to a simmer. Set aside to cool.

Place the ribs in a large saucepan, cover with water and bring to the boil. Reduce the heat and simmer for 15 minutes. Drain and set aside to cool slightly.

Cut the ribs between the bones and place in a large bowl. Pour over the marinade and toss to coat. Cover and refrigerate for at least 4 hours, or overnight.

Preheat the oven to 180°C (350°F/Gas 4). Line two baking trays with foil and set wire racks on top.

Remove the ribs from the marinade, reserving the marinade, and arrange on the wire racks. Cook in the oven, basting occasionally with the reserved marinade, for 40–50 minutes or until golden-brown.

Serve with steamed rice and garnish with spring onions.

# Gremolata-crumbed
# Veal Schnitzel

**Serves 4**

4 × 120 g (4 oz) veal loin steaks
3 tablespoons plain (all-purpose) flour
sea salt and freshly ground black pepper
2 large eggs, lightly beaten
40 g (1½ oz) butter
2 tablespoons olive oil
lemon wedges, to serve

### Gremolata Crumbs

1 loaf day-old, unsliced white bread, crust
   removed and bread roughly chopped
1 large handful flat-leaf (Italian)
   parsley, chopped
3 tablespoons finely grated parmesan
finely grated zest of 2 lemons
4 anchovy fillets, finely chopped

Lay the veal steaks between two sheets of baking paper and using a meat mallet flatten out to approximately 5 mm (¼ in) thick.

Preheat the oven to 120°C (250°F/ Gas ¼–½). Line a baking tray with paper towel.

To prepare the gremolata crumbs, spread the bread on a baking tray. Bake for 15– 20 minutes, turning occasionally, to dry out slightly; the bread should not be completely dry, just with a stale texture. Blend in batches in a food processor, until coarse. Transfer 2 cups of crumbs to a large bowl. Stir in the parsley, parmesan, lemon zest and anchovies and set aside. Store leftover crumbs in an airtight container in the refrigerator for up to 1 week.

Increase the oven temperature to 170°C (340°F/Gas 3).

To crumb the veal, coat the steaks in seasoned flour, dip in the egg and lastly coat in the gremolata crumbs, pressing gently to secure.

Melt half of the butter with half of the oil in a large frying pan over medium–high heat. Cook 1–2 schnitzels at a time, depending on the size of your pan, for 2 minutes on each side or until golden-brown. Transfer to the prepared tray and place in the oven to keep warm while you cook the remaining schnitzels.

Serve with lemon wedges.

# PRAWN AND CHORIZO PAELLA

**SERVES 4**

4 cups (1 litre/34 fl oz) chicken stock
pinch of saffron threads
3 tablespoons olive oil
2 chorizo sausages, sliced into rounds
1 onion, diced
3 garlic cloves, finely chopped
2 × 400 g (14 oz) tins whole tomatoes,
    drained
1 red capsicum (pepper), sliced
2 teaspoons smoked sweet paprika
2 cups (400 g/14 oz) medium-grain rice,
    such as calasparra, bomba or arborio
sea salt and freshly ground black pepper
400 g (14 oz) raw prawns (shrimp),
    peeled with tails left on
1 cup (125 g/4 oz) frozen peas
small handful flat-leaf (Italian)
    parsley, chopped
lemon wedges, to serve

Combine the stock and saffron threads in a saucepan and bring to the boil. Remove from the heat and set aside for 5 minutes, to infuse.

Heat 1 tablespoon of the oil in a paella pan or large frying pan over medium–high heat. Cook the chorizo until golden-brown. Transfer to a bowl and set aside.

Reduce the heat to low–medium, add the remaining oil to the pan and cook the onion and garlic, until softened. Add the drained tomatoes, capsicum and paprika and cook until the liquid has evaporated. Return the chorizo to the pan, add the rice and stir to combine. Pour in the infused stock and bring to the boil. Season with salt and pepper. Reduce the heat further to a gentle simmer, cover and cook, without stirring, for 15 minutes.

Arrange the prawns on top and scatter with peas, cover and cook for a further 5–10 minutes, until the rice is tender, the liquid has been absorbed and the prawns are cooked. Turn off the heat and leave to stand for 5 minutes before serving.

Sprinkle with parsley and serve with lemon wedges.

# Mussels with Tomato and Chilli

SERVES 4

1.5 kg (3 lb 5 oz) mussels,
  scrubbed clean and debearded
2 tablespoons olive oil
1 onion, diced
2 garlic cloves, finely chopped
1 long red chilli, deseeded and
  thinly sliced
2 small red bird's eye chillies,
  deseeded and thinly sliced
1 tablespoon tomato paste
  (concentrated tomato purée)
5 tomatoes, diced
½ cup (125 ml/4 fl oz) dry white wine
finely grated zest and juice of 1 lemon
1 small handful flat-leaf (Italian)
  parsley, chopped
crusty bread, to serve

Discard any broken mussels and tap any opened mussels gently on a work surface to ensure they are still alive. If they do not react and close, discard.

Heat the oil in a large saucepan over low–medium heat. Cook the onion, garlic and chillies, until softened. Add the tomato paste and tomato and stir to combine. Increase the heat to medium–high and add the mussels, white wine, and lemon zest and juice. Cover and cook, shaking the pan occasionally, for 4–6 minutes, or until the mussels have opened. Discard any mussels that haven't opened.

Sprinkle with parsley and toss through.

Serve with crusty bread.

# ● Soft Polenta with ●
# ● Mushrooms and Pesto ●

**Serves 4**

## Basil Pesto

**3 tablespoons pine nuts, lightly toasted**
**3 tablespoons coarsely grated parmesan**
**2 garlic cloves, coarsely chopped**
**2 large handfuls basil**
**1/2 cup (60 ml/2 fl oz) extra-virgin olive oil**

## Soft Polenta

**3 cups (750 ml/25 fl oz) chicken stock**
**1 cup (250 ml/8 1/2 fl oz) milk**
**1 cup (200 g/7 oz) instant polenta**
**1 cup (80 g/3 oz) finely grated parmesan**
**1/2 cup (125 g/4 oz) mascarpone**
**20 g (3/4 oz) butter, cubed**
**sea salt and freshly ground black pepper**

## Mushrooms

**40 g (1 1/2 oz) butter**
**4 French shallots, thinly sliced**
**2 garlic cloves, thinly sliced**
**600 g (1 lb 5 oz) mixed mushrooms,**
  **such as field, button, Swiss, pine**
  **and oyster, thickly sliced**
**juice of 1/2 lemon**
**sea salt and freshly ground black pepper**

To make the basil pesto, blend the pine nuts, parmesan and garlic together in a small food processor, to make a coarse paste. Add the basil and half the oil and blend, gradually adding the remaining oil, until combined. Transfer to a small bowl and set aside.

To make the soft polenta, combine the stock and milk in a heavy-based saucepan and bring to a simmer over medium heat. Gradually pour in the polenta in a thin and steady stream, whisking continuously, until incorporated. Reduce the heat to low and cook, stirring with a wooden spoon, for 10–15 minutes or until smooth and the polenta begins to come away from the side of the pan. Remove from the heat and stir in the parmesan, mascarpone and butter. Season with salt and pepper.

Meanwhile to prepare the mushrooms, melt the butter in a large frying pan over low–medium heat and cook the shallot and garlic, until softened. Add the mushrooms and cook for 3–4 minutes, until softened and golden-brown. Add the lemon juice and season with salt and pepper.

Serve the polenta topped with mushrooms and a dollop of pesto.

# RABBIT CACCIATORE

3 tablespoons olive oil
1.2 kg (2 lb 10 oz) farmed rabbit, jointed
  (ask your butcher to do this for you)
2 onions, sliced
1 carrot, diced
1 celery stalk, diced
3 garlic cloves, finely chopped
125 g (4 oz) button mushrooms, sliced
½ cup (125 ml/4 fl oz) dry white wine
½ cup (125 ml/4 fl oz) chicken stock
2 × 400 g (14 oz) tins whole tomatoes
1 sprig rosemary
1 bay leaf
1 cup (155 g/5 oz) pitted kalamata olives
sea salt and freshly ground black pepper
chopped flat-leaf (Italian) parsley,
  to serve

Heat the oil in a large heavy-based saucepan over medium–high heat. Cook the rabbit pieces in two batches for 2–3 minutes on each side, or until browned all over. Transfer to a plate and set aside.

Reduce the heat to low–medium and cook the onion, carrot, celery and garlic, until softened. Add the mushrooms and cook until golden-brown. Return the rabbit to the pan, pour in the wine and stock and bring to the boil. Add the tomatoes and their juice, squashing the tomatoes as you add them. Add the rosemary and bay leaf and stir to combine. Cover and gently simmer for 30 minutes. Add the olives, cover and gently simmer for a further 20–30 minutes, or until the meat is tender and starts to come away from the bone. Season with salt and pepper.

Serve sprinkled with parsley.

# Thai Beef and Noodle Salad

100 g (3½ oz) bean thread noodles

2 tablespoons vegetable or peanut oil

2 teaspoons red curry paste

500 g (1 lb 2 oz) beef fillet

2 Lebanese (short) cucumbers, halved
  lengthways and thinly sliced diagonally

250 g (9 oz) cherry tomatoes, halved

1 red capsicum (pepper), thinly
  sliced lengthways

½ red onion, thinly sliced

2 large handfuls mung bean sprouts

1 small handful mint

1 small handful coriander (cilantro)

1 small handful Thai basil

1 long red chilli, deseeded and
  thinly sliced

2 tablespoons roasted peanuts, chopped

### Dressing

2 tablespoons lime juice

1½ tablespoons fish sauce

1 tablespoon coarsely grated palm sugar
  (substitute soft brown sugar
  if unavailable)

2 teaspoons sesame oil

1 garlic clove, crushed

Place the noodles in a heatproof bowl, cover with boiling water and set aside for 5 minutes, to soften. Drain.

Heat the vegetable or peanut oil in a frying pan over medium–high heat.

Smear the curry paste over the beef. Sear the beef on all sides for 8–10 minutes, for medium, or until browned all over and cooked to your liking. Transfer to a plate, cover and set aside for 5 minutes, to rest.

Meanwhile to make the dressing, whisk the ingredients together in a small bowl, until the sugar dissolves.

Combine the noodles and the remaining salad ingredients, except the peanuts, in a large bowl. Thinly slice the beef and add to the salad. Pour over the dressing and toss to combine.

Serve sprinkled with peanuts.

# Slow-cooked Five-spice Pork Belly with Chinese Broccoli

Serves 4

1.2 kg (2 lb 10 oz) pork belly
2 teaspoons sea salt
1 teaspoon five-spice powder
1½ cups (375 ml/12½ fl oz) chicken stock
3 tablespoons dark soy sauce
2 tablespoons Shaoxing (Chinese)
  rice wine
1 tablespoon soft brown sugar
1 strip orange zest
½ cinnamon stick
1 star anise
1 teaspoon Sichuan peppercorns
steamed jasmine rice, to serve

### Chinese Broccoli

2 tablespoons chicken stock
1 tablespoon kecap manis
  (sweet soy sauce)
1 teaspoon cornflour (cornstarch)
1 tablespoon vegetable oil
1 garlic clove, thinly sliced
2.5 cm (1 in) piece ginger,
  peeled and finely shredded
2 bunches Chinese broccoli (gai lan),
  trimmed and cut in half

Score the pork skin at 2.5 cm (1 in) intervals. Combine the salt and five-spice powder and rub over the skin. Refrigerate for 1 hour.

Preheat the oven to 160°C (320°F/Gas 2–3).

Place the pork, skin-side up, in a baking tin. Combine the 1½ cups (375 ml/12½ fl oz) of stock and the remaining ingredients except the rice in a bowl and pour into the tray. Cover with foil and cook in the oven for 1½ hours.

Uncover the pork. Increase the oven temperature to 200°C (400°F/Gas 6) and cook for a further 30 minutes, or until the skin is crisp and the flesh tender. If the skin has not crisped sufficiently, place the pork under a griller (broiler) on high heat for a few minutes. Watch it carefully as it can burn easily. Set aside for 10 minutes, to rest.

Meanwhile, to prepare the Chinese broccoli, combine the 2 tablespoons of stock, kecap manis and cornflour in a small bowl.

Preheat a wok over high heat. Add the oil and swirl to coat. Add the garlic and ginger and cook for 10 seconds, or until fragrant. Add the broccoli and stir-fry for 1–2 minutes, or until the leaves are limp. Pour in the stock mixture and cook for a further minute, then toss to coat.

Remove the pork from its braising liquid and thickly slice. Serve with stir-fried Chinese broccoli and steamed jasmine rice.

# Moroccan Spiced Lamb Shanks with Date and Roasted Almond Couscous

3 tablespoons olive oil
4 large French-trimmed lamb shanks
⅓ cup (50 g/1¾ oz)
    plain (all-purpose) flour
sea salt and freshly ground black pepper
2 large onions, thinly sliced
1½ teaspoons ground ginger
1½ teaspoons ground cinnamon
1 teaspoon ground cumin
4 cups (1 litre/34 fl oz) chicken stock

Couscous
2 cups (400 g/14 oz) instant couscous
20 g (¾ oz) butter
2 tablespoons vegetable oil
½ cup (80 g/3 oz) blanched almonds
1 cup (200 g/7 oz) dates, pitted and sliced
1 small handful coriander (cilantro),
    chopped, plus extra whole leaves
    to serve
sea salt

Preheat the oven to 170°C (340°F/Gas 3).

Heat 2 tablespoons of the oil in a heavy-based ovenproof casserole dish over medium–high heat. Toss the lamb shanks in flour seasoned with salt and pepper and cook until the lamb is browned all over. Transfer to a plate.

Reduce the heat to low–medium, add the remaining oil to the dish and cook the onion, until softened. Add the spices and cook a further 30 seconds, or until fragrant. Return the shanks to the dish and add the stock. Cover and cook in the oven for 2 hours, or until the shanks are tender and the meat is almost falling off the bone.

To prepare the couscous, combine the couscous with 2 cups (500 ml/17 fl oz) boiling water and the butter in a medium-sized heatproof bowl. Cover with plastic wrap and set aside for 10 minutes.

Heat the oil in a small frying pan over medium heat. Add the almonds and cook for 2–3 minutes, or until golden-brown. Transfer to paper towel to drain.

Fluff the couscous with a fork to separate the grains. Add the almonds, dates and coriander, and stir to combine. Season with salt.

Serve the lamb shanks on a bed of couscous, spoon over some of the sauce and sprinkle with a little more coriander.

# — Chicken Tikka Masala —

4 skinless chicken breast fillets, cut into
   2.5 cm (1 in) pieces
steamed basmati rice, to serve
roti or naan bread, to serve

### Marinade
½ cup (125 g/4 oz) plain yoghurt
3 cm (1¼ in) piece ginger,
   peeled and finely grated
2 garlic cloves, crushed
2 teaspoons ground cumin
1 teaspoon ground cinnamon
1 teaspoon freshly ground black pepper
½ teaspoon chilli powder
½ teaspoon mild sweet paprika

### Sauce
2 tablespoons ghee or vegetable oil
1 onion, thinly sliced
2 garlic cloves, finely chopped
1 long red chilli, deseeded and
   finely chopped
2 teaspoons ground cumin
2 teaspoons mild sweet paprika
1 × 400 g (14 oz) tin chopped tomato
½ cup (125 g/4 oz) plain yoghurt
½ cup (125 ml/4 fl oz)
   pouring (whipping) cream
1 large handful coriander (cilantro),
   chopped

To make the marinade, combine all the ingredients in a medium-sized bowl. Add the chicken pieces and stir to coat. Cover and refrigerate overnight.

To make the sauce, heat the ghee in a large frying pan over low–medium heat. Add the onion, garlic, chilli, cumin and paprika and cook until the vegetables are softened and the mixture is fragrant. Add the chicken pieces and the marinade and toss to coat. Pour in the tomato and yoghurt and gently simmer for 10 minutes. Pour in the cream and simmer for a further 5 minutes, or until the sauce is thick and the chicken is cooked. Add the coriander and stir to combine.

Serve with steamed rice and roti or naan bread.

☞ This recipe needs to be prepared 1 day in advance.

# — Osso Bucco —

3 tablespoons olive oil

2 kg (4 lb 6 oz) osso bucco pieces
(centre-cut veal shank)

⅓ cup (50 g/1¾ oz) plain (all-purpose)
flour

sea salt and freshly ground black pepper

1 large onion, diced

2 celery stalks, diced

1 large carrot, diced

2 garlic cloves, finely chopped

2 cups (500 ml/17 fl oz) dry white wine

1 cup (250 ml/8½ fl oz) chicken stock

2 vine-ripened tomatoes, coarsely chopped

3 sprigs lemon thyme

2 bay leaves

zest of 1 lemon, cut into fine strips, to serve

2 tablespoons chopped flat-leaf (Italian)
parsley, to serve

Preheat the oven to 160°C (320°F/Gas 2–3).

Heat 2 tablespoons of the oil in an ovenproof casserole dish over medium–high heat.

Toss the veal pieces in the flour seasoned with salt and pepper then cook for 2–3 minutes on each side, until browned all over. Transfer to a plate.

Reduce the heat to low–medium, add the remaining oil to the dish and cook the onion, celery, carrot and garlic until softened and golden. Return the veal to the dish. Pour in the wine and stock and bring to the boil. Add the tomato, thyme and bay leaves. Cover and cook in the oven for 1½–2 hours, or until tender and the meat is almost falling off the bone. Remove from the oven and skim off any excess fat.

Serve sprinkled with lemon zest and parsley.

# KINGFISH NIÇOISE SALAD

4 × 150 g (5 oz) kingfish fillets
1 small handful flat-leaf (Italian) parsley,
    finely chopped
2 tablespoons capers, drained and rinsed,
    finely chopped
2 tablespoons olive oil
2 anchovy fillets, finely chopped
freshly ground black pepper
lemon wedges, to serve

### Niçoise Salad
8 new potatoes
4 large eggs
200 g (7 oz) green beans
150 g (5 oz) vine-ripened cherry
    tomatoes, halved
3 tablespoons niçoise (small black) olives
2 tablespoons white wine vinegar
1 tablespoon lemon juice
1 large egg yolk
1 garlic clove, crushed
1 teaspoon dijon mustard
½ cup (125 ml/4 fl oz) extra-virgin olive oil
sea salt and freshly ground black pepper

To prepare the fish, put the parsley, capers, oil and anchovies in a large bowl and stir to combine. Add the fish, season with pepper and toss to coat. Cover and refrigerate for 1 hour.

Meanwhile to prepare the salad, cook the potatoes in a small saucepan of boiling salted water for 8–10 minutes, or until tender. Drain and set aside to cool slightly. Slice thickly into rounds. Put the eggs in a small saucepan, cover with cold water, bring to the boil over medium heat and cook for 4 minutes. Drain and cool under cold running water for 1 minute. Peel and cut into wedges. Bring a saucepan of water to the boil then blanch the beans for 1 minute; drain and refresh in iced water. Combine the potato, egg, beans, tomato and olives in a large bowl.

To make the dressing, combine the vinegar, lemon juice, egg yolk, garlic and mustard in a small food processor and blend. Gradually add the oil in a thin, steady stream, blending until thick and creamy. Transfer to a small bowl and season with salt and pepper.

Preheat a char-grill, flat grill or large frying pan over medium–high heat.

Cook the fish for 2–3 minutes on each side or until cooked to your liking.

To serve, divide the salad among four serving plates, drizzle with the dressing and top with fish and lemon wedges.

Twice-cooked Chips

Creamy Roast Garlic
Potato Mash

Crumbed Cheesy
Polenta Chips

Brussels Sprouts
with Pancetta and
Roasted Walnuts

Button Mushrooms
Sautéed with
Garlic and Herbs

Fattoush

Asparagus with Lemon
and Parmesan

Glazed Dill
Baby Carrots

Broad Bean,
Pancetta and
Feta Salad

Greek Salad

Coleslaw

Baby Beetroot
and Orange Salad

Potato Salad

Macaroni and
Four Cheeses

Onion Rings

# — TWICE-COOKED CHIPS —

**1 kg (2 lb 3 oz) large all-purpose potatoes, such as sebago**
**vegetable oil, for deep-frying**
**sea salt**

Peel the potatoes and rinse under cold water. Cut into 1.5 cm (⁵⁄₈ in) thick chips. Place in a large bowl and cover with cold water. Leave to soak for 30 minutes.

Drain the chips and spread out on clean tea towels. Pat dry.

Two-thirds fill a deep-fryer or a large heavy-based saucepan with vegetable oil and heat to 150°C (300°F).

Partially cook the chips in batches, for 5 minutes. Remove using a slotted spoon and put on paper towel to drain.

Heat the oil to 190°C (375°F).

Fry the chips for a second time, again in batches (so as to not cool the oil down too much, which will cause the chips to become greasy) for 5 minutes, or until golden-brown and crisp, yet still fluffy on the inside. Remove using a slotted spoon and spread on paper towel to drain. Season with salt.

# CREAMY ROAST GARLIC — POTATO MASH

1 bulb garlic
olive oil, for drizzling
1 kg (2 lb 3 oz) all-purpose potatoes,
    such as sebago or desiree
½ cup (125 ml/4 fl oz) pouring (whipping)
    cream
100 g (3½ oz) butter
sea salt and ground white pepper

Preheat the oven to 180°C (350°F/Gas 4).

Place the whole garlic bulb on a baking tray and drizzle with oil. Roast in the oven for 30–40 minutes, until very soft. Set aside to cool slightly.

Peel and halve the potatoes and place in a large saucepan of cold salted water. Cover and bring to the boil over high heat. Uncover and boil for 15 minutes, or until tender when tested with a skewer. Drain and return to the pan. Mash using a potato masher. Press the mash through a sieve or fine strainer into a bowl, using the back of a spoon to push the potato through.

Heat the cream and butter together in a small saucepan over medium heat, until the butter has melted and the cream is hot. Pour into the potato and using a wooden spoon, beat to combine.

Cut the base off the roasted garlic bulb and squeeze out the softened cloves starting from the tip and pressing down. Add to the potato and beat to combine. Season with salt and white pepper.

# Crumbed Cheesy Polenta Chips

1½ cups (375 ml/12½ fl oz) chicken stock
1 cup (250 ml/8½ fl oz) full-cream milk
¾ cup (150 g/5 oz) instant polenta
½ cup (40 g/1½ oz) finely grated parmesan
20 g (¾ oz) butter, cubed
sea salt and freshly ground black pepper
1 large egg
2 tablespoons milk
⅓ cup (50 g/1¾ oz) plain (all-purpose) flour
2 cups (160 g/5½ oz) fresh breadcrumbs

Lightly grease a 28 cm × 20 cm (11 in × 8 in) tray and line with baking paper.

Combine the stock and milk in a heavy-based saucepan and bring to a simmer over medium heat. Gradually pour in the polenta in a thin steady stream, whisking continuously until incorporated. Reduce the heat to low and cook, stirring with a wooden spoon, for 10–15 minutes, or until the polenta is smooth and begins to come away from the sides of the pan. Remove from the heat and stir in the parmesan and butter. Season with salt and pepper.

Pour the polenta into the prepared tray. Place a sheet of baking paper on top and spread out the polenta to create a smooth even surface. Set aside for 15 minutes, to cool slightly. Refrigerate for at least 2 hours or overnight, until set.

Two-thirds fill a deep-fryer or a large, deep, heavy-based saucepan with vegetable oil and heat to 190°C (375°F).

Slice the polenta into 1.5 cm (⅝ in) thick chips. Beat the egg and milk together in a medium-sized bowl and place the flour and breadcrumbs in separate bowls. Coat the polenta chips in flour, then egg and finally crumbs, pressing gently to secure.

Fry the chips in batches for 2–3 minutes, or until crisp and golden. Remove using a slotted spoon and place on paper towel to drain. Season with salt.

# — Brussels Sprouts with —
## — Pancetta and Roasted Walnuts —

400 g (14 oz) brussels sprouts
1 tablespoon olive oil
100 g (3½ oz) pancetta, sliced thinly and
   cut into 1.5 cm (⅝ in) pieces
1 onion, sliced
4 garlic cloves, thinly sliced
⅓ cup (80 ml/3 fl oz) chicken stock
juice of ½ lemon
1 tablespoon (20 g/¾ oz) butter
½ cup (60 g/2 oz) walnut halves

Preheat the oven to 180°C (350°F/Gas 4).

Remove the outer brussels sprout leaves if very dark, and trim the bases.

Heat the oil in a heavy-based saucepan over medium heat. Add the pancetta and cook for 2–3 minutes or until golden-brown. Add the onion and garlic and cook until softened. Add the sprouts and toss to combine. Pour in the stock and lemon juice. Add the butter and bring to a gentle simmer. Cover and cook over low heat for 10 minutes.

Meanwhile put the walnuts on a baking tray and roast in the oven for 5–8 minutes, or until golden-brown.

Remove the lid from the Brussels sprouts and simmer for a further 10 minutes, or until the sprouts are just tender and the liquid has almost completely evaporated. Add the walnuts and toss to combine.

# Button Mushrooms Sautéed with Garlic and Herbs

500 g (1 lb 2 oz) button mushrooms,
   stalks trimmed
2 tablespoons olive oil
4 garlic cloves, thinly sliced
1 tablespoon red wine vinegar
1 tablespoon (20 g/¾ oz) butter
½ bunch chives, trimmed and cut into
   5 cm (2 in) lengths
sea salt and freshly ground black pepper

Wipe the mushrooms with damp paper towel to remove any dirt.

Heat the oil in a large frying pan over low–medium heat. Add the garlic and cook until softened. Add the mushrooms and cook for 5 minutes, or until golden-brown. Add the vinegar and butter and toss to coat. Add the chives and toss to combine. Season with salt and pepper.

# Fattoush

**Serves 4**

2 vine-ripened tomatoes, diced
2 Lebanese (short) cucumbers, diced
½ red capsicum (pepper), diced
½ green capsicum (pepper), diced
4 small radishes, cut into thin wedges
4 spring onions (scallions), sliced
1 large handful flat-leaf (Italian) parsley,
  coarsely chopped
1 large handful mint, coarsely chopped
1 large pita bread
olive oil, for brushing
½ teaspoon sumac

LEMON AND SUMAC DRESSING
2 tablespoons lemon juice
2 teaspoons sumac
1 garlic clove, crushed
⅓ cup (80 ml/3 fl oz) extra-virgin olive oil
sea salt and freshly ground black pepper

Combine the tomato, cucumber, red and green capsicum, radish, spring onion, parsley and mint in a medium-sized bowl.

Preheat a large frying pan over medium heat. Lightly brush the pita bread with oil and sprinkle with sumac. Cook for 1 minute on each side or until crisp and golden-brown. Break into small pieces.

To make the dressing, combine the lemon juice, sumac and garlic in a small bowl. Gradually whisk in the oil and season with salt and pepper.

Add the dressing and the bread to the salad and toss to coat. Serve immediately so the bread remains crisp.

# Asparagus with Lemon and Parmesan

2 bunches asparagus
20 g (¾ oz) butter
finely grated zest of 1 lemon
sea salt and freshly ground black pepper
30 g (1 oz) shaved parmesan

Preheat the oven to 180°C (350°F/Gas 4).

Trim and discard the woody ends of the asparagus.

Cut 2 pieces of foil and overlap a large baking tray. Spread the asparagus out over the foil, dot with the butter and scatter with the lemon zest. Season with salt and pepper.

Bring the foil edges together to make a parcel and fold over to completely seal. Bake for 10–15 minutes, or until the asparagus is just tender.

Transfer to a serving plate and scatter with the parmesan.

Serve hot.

# Glazed Dill Baby Carrots

SERVES 4

2 bunches baby (Dutch) carrots
1 tablespoon (20 g/³⁄₄ oz) butter
1 tablespoon soft brown sugar
3 tablespoons chicken stock
2 tablespoons chopped dill

Trim the carrots and wash thoroughly.

Melt the butter and sugar together over low heat in a large frying pan with a fitted lid. Pour in the stock and bring to a simmer. Add the carrots, cover and cook, shaking the pan occasionally to help the carrots cook evenly, for 5 minutes. Remove the lid and cook, tossing to coat, for 5 minutes, or until the carrots are tender and the liquid has reduced to a glaze. Add the dill and toss to coat.

Serve hot.

# Broad Bean, Pancetta and Feta Salad

**Serves 4**

400 g (14 oz) podded fresh or frozen
broad (fava) beans, approximately 1.2 kg
(2 lb 10 oz) unpodded
10 thin slices mild pancetta
80 g (3 oz) baby spinach leaves
1 large handful mint
100 g (3½ oz) soft goat's milk feta

LEMON DRESSING
2 tablespoons lemon juice
1 garlic clove, crushed
½ teaspoon sugar
⅓ cup (80 ml/3 fl oz) extra-virgin olive oil
sea salt and freshly ground black pepper

Bring a large saucepan of salted water to the boil. Cook the broad beans for 6 minutes, or until tender. Drain and refresh under cold running water. Remove and discard the skins.

Preheat a large frying pan over low–medium heat. Cook the pancetta for 4–5 minutes, or until very crisp and golden-brown.

To make the dressing, combine the lemon juice, garlic and sugar in a small bowl. Gradually whisk in the oil and season with salt and pepper.

Combine the pancetta, broad beans, spinach and mint in a medium-sized bowl. Add knobs of feta and pour over the dressing. Toss to coat.

# Greek Salad

SERVES 4

3 vine-ripened tomatoes
2 Lebanese (short) cucumbers
½ green capsicum (pepper), diced
⅓ cup (80 g/3½ oz) pitted kalamata olives
100 g (3½ oz) feta, cubed
½ red onion, thinly sliced
1 large handful flat-leaf (Italian) parsley, chopped
2 tablespoons red wine vinegar
1 teaspoon dried oregano
1 garlic clove, crushed
⅓ cup (80 ml/3 fl oz) extra-virgin olive oil
sea salt and freshly ground black pepper

Cut the tomatoes into wedges and place in a large bowl.

Cut the cucumbers in half lengthways and slice crossways 1 cm (⅜ in) thick.

Combine the tomato, cucumber, capsicum, olives, feta, onion and parsley in a large bowl.

Combine the vinegar, oregano and garlic in a small bowl. Gradually whisk in the oil and season with salt and pepper.

Add the dressing to the salad and toss to coat.

# Coleslaw

¼ white cabbage
¼ red cabbage
2 carrots
1 red onion, thinly sliced
2 large handfuls flat-leaf (Italian) parsley,
   chopped
2 large egg yolks
2 tablespoons cider vinegar
2 teaspoons dijon mustard
½ teaspoon sugar
1 cup (250 ml/8½ fl oz) light olive oil
sea salt and freshly ground black pepper

Finely shred the white and red cabbages and place in a large bowl.

Peel and cut the carrots in half crossways. Thinly slice into lengths and then slice into thin strips. Add the carrot, onion and parsley to the cabbage.

Whisk the egg yolks, vinegar, mustard and sugar together in a medium-sized bowl. Gradually pour in the oil, whisking continuously, until thick. Season with salt and pepper. Add to the salad and toss to combine.

# — Baby Beetroot —
# — and Orange Salad —

2 bunches baby beetroot
60 g (2 oz) baby beetroot leaves,
   or rocket (arugula)
1 orange
1 tablespoon red wine vinegar
3 tablespoons extra-virgin olive oil
sea salt and freshly ground black pepper
1 small handful dill, chopped
½ cup (125 g/4 oz) crème fraîche

Trim the ends off the beetroot. Pick the small leaves, wash and combine with the other leaves.

Bring a large saucepan of salted water to the boil. Cook the unpeeled beetroot for 20–25 minutes, or until tender. Drain and set aside, until they are cool enough to handle.

Wearing food-handling gloves, to prevent staining your hands, rub the skins off the beetroot. Cut into wedges and place in a medium-sized bowl.

Finely grate the zest of the orange into a small bowl.

Trim the ends off the orange and using a small sharp knife, cut off the peel and pith. Segment the orange and add the segments to the beetroot. Squeeze the remaining orange pulp over the bowl with the zest, to catch the juice.

Add the vinegar to the orange juice and zest and gradually whisk in the oil. Season with salt and pepper. Pour over the beetroot and orange, add the dill and toss to combine.

To serve, top with crème fraîche and freshly ground black pepper.

# — Potato Salad —

Serves 4

600 g (1 lb 5 oz) new potatoes, unpeeled
2 large eggs
8 slices mild pancetta
½ bunch chives, trimmed and cut into
   5 cm (2 in) lengths
1 tablespoon capers, rinsed and chopped

Crème Fraîche Dressing
½ cup (125 g/4 oz) crème fraîche
1 tablespoon lemon juice
2 teaspoons seeded mustard
sea salt and freshly ground black pepper

Place the potatoes in a large saucepan, cover with cold salted water and bring to the boil. Reduce the heat and simmer for 10 minutes, or until tender when pierced with a skewer. Drain.

Place the eggs in a small saucepan, cover with cold water and bring to the boil over high heat. Reduce the heat and gently simmer for 7 minutes. Drain and cool under cold running water for 1 minute. Peel and cut into wedges. Set aside.

Preheat a large frying pan over low–medium heat. Cook the pancetta for 4–5 minutes, or until very crisp and golden-brown. Transfer onto paper towel, to drain.

To make the crème fraîche dressing, whisk the crème fraîche, lemon juice and mustard together in a small bowl. Season with salt and pepper.

Combine the potatoes, egg, pancetta, chives and capers in a large bowl. Add the dressing and toss to coat.

# MACARONI AND FOUR CHEESES

300 g (10½ oz) dried macaroni
1 tablespoon olive oil
20 g (¾ oz) butter
1 small onion, diced
2 tablespoons plain (all-purpose) flour
½ cup (125 ml/4 fl oz) pouring
  (whipping) cream
1½ cups (375 ml/12½ fl oz) milk
1 cup (250 ml/8½ fl oz) mascarpone
100 g (3½ oz) cheddar, coarsely grated
100 g (3½ oz) gruyère, coarsely grated
½ teaspoon ground nutmeg
sea salt and freshly ground black pepper
1 cup (80 g/3 oz) fresh breadcrumbs
40 g (1½ oz) parmesan, coarsely grated

Preheat the oven to 180°C (350°F/Gas 4).

Bring a large saucepan of salted water to the boil over high heat. Add the macaroni and cook until *al dente*. Drain.

Heat the oil and butter in a large saucepan over low–medium heat and cook the onion until soft. Add the flour and cook for 1 minute. Gradually pour in the cream and the milk, stirring continuously with a wooden spoon. Bring to the boil then decrease the heat to low and simmer for 3–5 minutes until thickened. Remove from the heat and stir in the mascarpone, cheddar and gruyère. Season with nutmeg, and salt and pepper.

Add the macaroni to the cheese sauce and stir to combine. Pour into an ovenproof dish approximately 20 cm (8 in) square and sprinkle the top with the breadcrumbs and parmesan.

Bake in the oven for 20–25 minutes, or until crisp and golden-brown.

# — Onion Rings —

3 large onions
1 cup (150 g/5 oz) plain (all-purpose) flour,
    plus extra for coating
½ teaspoon baking powder
⅓ cup (80 ml/3 fl oz) milk
20 g (¾ oz) butter, melted
¾ cup (180 ml/6 fl oz) beer or soda water
vegetable oil, for deep-frying
sea salt

Peel and slice the onions into 1 cm (³⁄₈ in) thick rounds. Push the centre rings out and separate the remaining rounds into rings.

Sift the flour and baking powder together into a large bowl. Make a well in the centre and pour in the milk and butter, mixing in a little of the flour to combine. Pour in the beer or soda water and whisk, until smooth.

Two-thirds fill a deep-fryer or a large, deep, heavy-based saucepan with vegetable oil and heat to 190°C (375°F).

Toss the onion rings in flour and dredge in the batter. Cook in batches, for 1–2 minutes on each side, or until crisp and golden-brown. Drain on paper towel. Season with salt.

Eton Mess

Apple Pie

Lemon Meringue Pie

Chocolate Stout Puddings

Lime Delicious

Mud Cake

Sticky Date Pudding

Crème Brûlée

Bread and Butter Pudding

Bakewell Tart

# ⏤ Eton Mess ⏤

450 g (1 lb) strawberries,
   hulled and quartered
3 tablespoons caster (superfine) sugar
²⁄₃ cup (160 ml/5 ½ fl oz) pouring
   (whipping) cream
½ cup (125 g/4 oz) crème fraîche
2 tablespoons icing (confectioners') sugar
¼ teaspoon vanilla extract

MERINGUES
2 large egg whites
¼ teaspoon cream of tartar
²⁄₃ cup (145 g/5 oz) caster (superfine) sugar

Preheat the oven to 120°C (250°F/ Gas ¼–½). Line two baking trays with baking paper.

To make the meringues, whisk the egg whites using an electric mixer with a whisk attachment, until soft peaks form. Add the cream of tartar and gradually add the sugar, whisking continuously to make a thick glossy meringue.

Spoon the meringue onto the prepared baking trays, making six approximately 8 cm (3¼ in) wide mounds. Bake in the oven for 50–60 minutes, until crisp but not coloured. Turn the oven off, set the door ajar and leave the meringues overnight to dry out.

Place half of the strawberries in a bowl and roughly mash using a potato masher. Add the remaining strawberries and the sugar, stir and set aside for 15 minutes, or until the juices begin to seep and the strawberries soften slightly.

Whip the cream, crème fraîche, icing sugar and vanilla together using an electric mixer with a whisk attachment, until soft peaks form.

Roughly crush the meringues. Place the cream mixture and half of the meringues and half of the strawberries in a medium-sized bowl and stir until just combined. To assemble, create layers of crushed meringue, strawberries and the mixed strawberry cream in four serving glasses.

☞ This recipe needs to be prepared the day before. Alternatively use store-bought meringues for a quick and easy dessert.

# — APPLE PIE —

melted butter, for greasing
1 large egg, lightly beaten, for glazing
1 tablespoon raw (demerara) sugar,
    for sprinkling
cream or ice cream, to serve

SWEET SHORTCRUST PASTRY
2 ½ cups (375 g/13 oz) plain
    (all-purpose) flour
3 tablespoons icing (confectioners') sugar
150 g (5 oz) butter, chilled and diced
1 large egg yolk

FILLING
8 granny smith apples, peeled,
    quartered and thickly sliced
juice of 1 lemon
60 g (2 oz) butter
½ cup (110 g/3 ¾ oz) caster
    (superfine) sugar
1 teaspoon ground cinnamon
½ teaspoon ground cloves
½ cup (40 g/1 ½ oz) fresh breadcrumbs

To make the pastry, place the flour and icing sugar in a food processor and pulse to combine. Add the butter and pulse, until the mixture resembles fine crumbs. Lightly beat the egg yolk with ⅓ cup (80 ml/3 fl oz) chilled water in a small bowl. Add to the crumb mixture and pulse to incorporate. The mixture will look dry and crumbly. Turn out onto a clean work surface, gently knead and shape into two discs, one using two-thirds of the dough and the other the remaining third. Do not overwork. Wrap in plastic wrap and refrigerate for 30 minutes.

Lightly grease a 4 cm (1½ in) deep, 28 cm × 25 cm (11 in × 10 in) pie dish with butter.

Roll the larger dough disc out between two sheets of baking paper, to 3 mm (⅛ in) thick. Line the prepared dish and trim the edges. Roll the remaining dough out between two sheets of baking paper, so it is large enough to cover the top of the pie. Lay flat on a tray and cut a 3 cm (1¼ in) circle out of the centre. Refrigerate the pie dish and the pastry disc for 20 minutes.

Preheat the oven to 200°C (400°F/ Gas 6).

Meanwhile, to prepare the filling, place the apple in a medium-sized bowl and toss in the lemon juice, to prevent browning. Melt the butter in a large saucepan over medium heat. Add the apple, sugar and spices, and cook, stirring occasionally, for 3–5 minutes or until just softened. Strain the fruit, reserving the juices. Return the juices to the pan and simmer for 1–2 minutes, until thickened slightly to a syrup. Add the syrup and breadcrumbs to the apple and stir to combine. Set aside to cool.

Spoon the filling into the pie base. Lay the remaining sheet of pastry on top, trim off the excess and pinch the edges together to secure. Brush with the egg and sprinkle with the raw sugar.

Place the pie on a flat baking tray and bake in the oven for 45–50 minutes, until the pastry is golden-brown.

Slice and serve hot with cream or ice cream.

# — LEMON MERINGUE PIE —

**1 quantity Sweet Shortcrust Pastry (see opposite)**

### LEMON CURD FILLING
**finely grated zest and juice of 3 lemons**
**1 cup (220 g/8 oz) caster (superfine) sugar**
**3 tablespoons cornflour (cornstarch)**
**4 large egg yolks**
**80 g (3 oz) butter, cubed**

### MERINGUE TOPPING
**1¼ cups (275 g/10 oz) caster (superfine) sugar**
**4 large egg whites**

Lightly grease and flour one 23 cm (9 in) fluted tart pan with a removable base. Roll the pastry dough between two sheets of baking paper, to 5 mm (¼ in) thick. Line the prepared pan with pastry. Trim the edges and refrigerate for 20 minutes.

Preheat the oven to 190°C (375°F/ Gas 5).

Place the tart on a baking tray and prick the base of the pastry with a fork. Line with baking paper and fill with baking weights, dried beans or uncooked rice. Blind bake for 15 minutes, or until the edges begin to turn light golden. Remove the baking paper and weights and cook for a further 5–10 minutes, until the base is golden and the pastry is cooked through. Set aside to cool.

Increase the oven temperature to 200°C (400°F/Gas 6).

To make the filling, combine the lemon juice and zest and the sugar with 1 cup (250 ml/8½ fl oz) water in a saucepan over low heat and gently simmer for 3–5 minutes, until the sugar dissolves. Blend the cornflour and 2 tablespoons cold water together in a heatproof bowl. Gradually stir in the lemon liquid. Return to the saucepan and cook over low–medium heat, stirring constantly to prevent lumps, for 3–5 minutes, or until thick. Whisk in the egg yolks and butter. Transfer to a bowl and set aside to cool. Pour the filling into the pastry case. Cover and refrigerate until cold and set.

To make the meringue topping, combine the sugar and ⅓ cup (80 ml/3 fl oz) water in a saucepan over low heat. Simmer for 3 minutes or until the sugar dissolves. Whisk the egg whites until soft peaks form. Pour in the sugar syrup in a thin steady stream, whisking continuously to make a thick glossy meringue. Spoon on top of the lemon base and use a spatula or the back of a spoon to create small peaks.

Bake the pie on the top shelf of the oven for 5 minutes, or until the meringue peaks are golden. Set on a wire rack to cool completely. Slice to serve.

# — CHOCOLATE STOUT PUDDINGS —

1 cup (150 g/5 oz) self-raising flour

⅓ cup (75 g/2 ½ oz) caster (superfine) sugar

⅓ cup (50 g/1¾ oz) unsweetened cocoa powder

½ cup (125 ml/4 fl oz) milk

50 g (1¾ oz) unsalted butter, melted

1 large egg, lightly beaten

50 g (1¾ oz) dark chocolate, coarsely grated

⅔ cup firmly packed (150 g/5 oz) dark brown sugar

1½ cups (375 ml/12 ½ fl oz) stout beer

cream or ice cream, to serve

Preheat the oven to 180°C (350°F/Gas 4). Lightly grease six 1 cup (250 ml/8 ½ fl oz) ovenproof ramekins.

Sift the flour, caster sugar and half of the cocoa powder together into a medium-sized bowl. Add the milk, melted butter and egg and mix well. Add the chocolate and stir to combine. Spoon the batter into the prepared ramekins.

Combine the remaining cocoa powder with the brown sugar and sprinkle over the top of the puddings.

Combine the stout and ¾ cup (180 ml/6 fl oz) water in a small saucepan and bring to the boil over high heat. Pour over the pudding batter.

Place the ramekins in a baking tray and pour enough boiling water into the tray to come halfway up the sides of the ramekins. Bake in the oven for 15–20 minutes, or until risen and firm to the touch.

Serve hot with cream or ice cream.

# LIME DELICIOUS

½ cup (110 g/3 ¾ oz) caster (superfine) sugar
50 g (1 ¾ oz) butter, softened, plus additional, melted, for greasing
finely grated zest and juice of 3 limes
2 large eggs, separated
3 tablespoons self-raising flour
1 cup (250 ml/8 ½ fl oz) milk
icing (confectioners') sugar, for dusting
cream or ice cream, to serve

Preheat the oven to 180°C (350°F/Gas 4). Lightly grease four 1 cup (250 ml/8 ½ fl oz) ovenproof ramekins or one 4 cup (1 litre/34 fl oz) ovenproof dish.

Cream the sugar, softened butter and lime zest together in a medium-sized bowl, until pale and creamy. Add the egg yolks, one at a time, mixing to combine. Add the lime juice, flour and milk, a little at a time, and stir to combine.

In a separate bowl, whisk the egg whites, using an electric mixer with a whisk attachment, until soft peaks form. Stir 1 large spoonful of egg whites into the batter. Gently fold in the remaining egg whites.

Divide the mixture evenly among the prepared ramekins or spoon it into the dish. Place the ramekins or dish in a deep baking tray and pour enough boiling water into the tray to come halfway up the sides.

Bake in the oven for 25–30 minutes for the ramekins, 40–45 minutes for the dish, or until puffed and golden.

Dust with icing sugar and serve hot with cream or ice cream.

# — MUD CAKE —

250 g (9 oz) butter, coarsely chopped

250 g (9 oz) dark chocolate, 70% cocoa, coarsely chopped

2 shots (60 ml/2 fl oz) espresso coffee

1½ cups (330 g/11 ½ oz) caster (superfine) sugar

2 large eggs, lightly beaten

1⅔ cup (250 g/9 oz) plain (all-purpose) flour

3 tablespoons unsweetened cocoa powder

1 teaspoon baking powder

1 cup (250 ml/8 ½ fl oz) buttermilk

cream, to serve (optional)

### CHOCOLATE CURLS

200 g (7 oz) white chocolate melts (buttons)

200 g (7 oz) dark chocolate melts (buttons)

### GÂNACHE

250 g (9 oz) dark chocolate, 70% solids, coarsely chopped

½ cup (125 ml/4 fl oz) pouring (whipping) cream

40 g (1½ oz) butter, cubed

Preheat the oven to 160°C (320°F/ Gas 2–3). Lightly grease a 22 cm (8½ in) round springform cake pan and line the base and sides with baking paper.

Place the butter, dark chocolate and coffee in a heatproof bowl and set over a saucepan of barely simmering water to melt, stirring occasionally, until smooth. Remove from the heat, add the sugar and the eggs and stir to combine. Sift the flour, cocoa powder and baking powder over the chocolate mixture. Add the buttermilk and mix well. Pour the mixture into the prepared pan and smooth over the centre, to help prevent it from rising unevenly.

Bake for 1 hour and 15 minutes, or until a skewer comes out clean when tested. Set aside to cool in the pan.

To make the chocolate curls, melt the white and dark chocolate in separate bowls, over a saucepan of barely simmering water. Make sure the bowls do not touch the water. Pour onto a glass or marble surface, keeping the two chocolates separate, and put aside until the chocolate is set but not hard.

Push a large kitchen knife set at a 45 degree angle away from you, across the surface of the chocolate to form curls. Transfer the curls onto a tray and set aside in a cool place.

To make the gânache, place the chocolate, cream and butter in a heatproof bowl and set over a saucepan of barely simmering water to melt, stirring occasionally, until smooth. Make sure the bowl does not touch the water. Remove the bowl from the heat and set aside for 20 minutes, or until cooled.

To glaze the cake, remove the cooled cake from the pan and set on a wire rack. Pour the gânache over the centre of the cake and using a spatula, smooth over the surface and around the sides. Put aside for 10 minutes to set slightly. Decorate with white and dark chocolate curls.

Slice and serve with cream, if desired.

# ⸺ Sticky Date Pudding ⸺

2 cups (400 g/14 oz) pitted dates,
  coarsely chopped
80 g (3 oz) dark chocolate
1 teaspoon bicarbonate of soda
¾ cup firmly packed (165 g/5 ½ oz)
  dark brown sugar
80 g (3 oz) unsalted butter, softened
2 large eggs
1 cup (150 g/5 oz) self-raising flour
1 teaspoon mixed spice
cream or ice cream, to serve

BUTTERSCOTCH SAUCE
1½ cups firmly packed (345 g/12 oz)
  dark brown sugar
1 cup (250 ml/8 ½ fl oz) pouring
  (whipping) cream
150 g (5 oz) unsalted butter

Preheat the oven to 180°C (350°F/ Gas 4). Lightly grease an 18 cm (7 in) square baking pan and line the base and sides with baking paper.

Combine the dates, chocolate, bicarbonate of soda and 1 cup (250 ml/8½ fl oz) boiling water in a medium-sized heatproof bowl. Set aside for 10 minutes, for the dates to soften and the chocolate to melt.

Cream the sugar and butter together in a medium-sized bowl, until pale and creamy. Add the eggs, one at a time, mixing to combine. Stir in the date mixture. Sift the flour and mixed spice over the top and fold through. Spoon the mixture into the prepared pan.

Bake for 30–35 minutes, or until risen and a skewer comes out clean when tested.

Meanwhile, to make the butterscotch sauce, combine the sugar, cream and butter in a small saucepan over low–medium heat. Simmer for 5–10 minutes, or until the butter has melted, sugar has dissolved and the sauce has thickened. Strain into a jug.

Cut the pudding into portions and serve hot with butterscotch sauce and cream or ice cream.

☞ For individual puddings, lightly grease eight ¾ cup (180 ml/6 fl oz) capacity muffin pan holes and line with baking paper. Half fill with mixture and bake for 15 minutes.

# — Crème Brûlée —

**Serves 4**

2 ½ cups (625 ml/21 fl oz) thickened
   (whipping) cream
1 vanilla bean, split in half lengthways,
   seeds scraped
6 large egg yolks
½ cup (110 g/3 ¾ oz) caster
   (superfine) sugar

Preheat the oven to 120°C (250°F/ Gas ¼–½). Line a deep baking tray with a folded tea towel and arrange four 200 ml (7 fl oz) ovenproof ramekins on top.

Place the cream and vanilla bean and seeds in a small saucepan over low–medium heat and bring to scalding point.

Whisk the egg yolks and half of the sugar together in a medium-sized bowl, until pale and creamy. Gradually add the hot cream, stirring to combine. Strain through a fine-mesh sieve into a jug.

Divide the custard mixture evenly among the ramekins. Pour enough boiling water into the tray to come halfway up the sides of the ramekins. Cover the tray loosely with foil, so air can still circulate through.

Bake in the oven for 40 minutes, or until the custards have just set: they will still have a slight wobble in the centre.

Remove the ramekins from the tray and set aside to cool. Cover with plastic wrap and refrigerate for 4 hours or overnight.

Before serving, take the crème brûlées out of the refrigerator for 20 minutes, to take the chill off the cream.

Sprinkle the remaining caster sugar evenly over the custards. Caramelise the sugar by either using a kitchen blowtorch or placing under a hot grill (broiler), until dark brown.

# Bread and Butter Pudding

100 g (3 ½ oz) sultanas (golden raisins)

3 tablespoons brandy

12 x 1 cm (³/₈ in) thick slices sourdough
   bread

80 g (3 oz) butter, softened,
   plus extra for greasing

⅓ cup (105 g/3 ¾ oz) orange marmalade

6 large eggs

3 tablespoons caster (superfine) sugar

1 teaspoon vanilla extract

½ teaspoon ground cinnamon

1 cup (250 ml/8 ½ fl oz) milk

1 cup (250 ml/8 ½ fl oz) pouring
   (whipping) cream

3 tablespoons raw (demerara) sugar

cream or ice cream, to serve (optional)

Lightly grease a 2 litre (64 fl oz) casserole dish with butter.

Place the sultanas and brandy in a small bowl and set aside for 10 minutes, to plump.

Smear the bread with the butter and marmalade and cut in half diagonally, to create triangles.

Arrange the bread slices, in overlapping layers, in the prepared dish, scattering the brandied sultanas between each layer.

Whisk the eggs, sugar, vanilla and cinnamon together in a medium-sized bowl. Add the milk and cream and whisk to combine. Pour over the bread slices and set aside for 45 minutes, or until the custard mixture has been absorbed.

Preheat the oven to 180°C (350°F/Gas 4).

Sprinkle the pudding with raw sugar and bake for 30–40 minutes, until golden-brown and the custard is firm.

Cut into portions and serve with cream or ice cream, if desired.

# — BAKEWELL TART —

SERVES 8–10

icing (confectioners') sugar, for dusting
whipped cream, to serve

### SWEET SHORTCRUST PASTRY
1¼ cups (185 g/6½ oz) plain
   (all-purpose) flour
⅓ cup (35 g/1 oz) ground almonds
2 tablespoons icing (confectioners') sugar
125 g (4 oz) unsalted butter,
   chilled and cubed
1 large egg yolk

### FILLING
125 g (4 oz) unsalted butter, softened
¾ cup (160 g/5½ oz) caster
   (superfine) sugar
finely grated zest of ½ lemon
3 large eggs
1½ cups (150 g/5 oz) ground almonds
3 tablespoons plain (all-purpose) flour
⅓ cup (105 g/3¾ oz) raspberry jam
3 tablespoons flaked almonds

To make the pastry, put the flour, ground almonds and icing sugar in a food processor and pulse to combine. Add the butter and pulse, until the mixture resembles fine crumbs. Lightly beat the egg yolk with 2 tablespoons chilled water in a small bowl. Add to the crumb mixture and pulse, until just combined. Do not overwork. Turn out onto a clean work surface and shape the dough to form a disc. Wrap in plastic wrap and refrigerate for 30 minutes. Alternatively, to make the dough by hand, rub the butter into the flour in a medium-sized bowl and mix in the yolk mixture.

Grease and flour a 23 cm (9 in) tart pan with removable base.

Roll the dough out between two sheets of baking paper, to 5 mm (¼ in) thick. Line the prepared pan with pastry. Trim the edges and refrigerate for 20 minutes.

Preheat the oven to 190°C (375°F/Gas 5).

Place the tart on a baking tray and prick the base of the pastry with a fork. Line with baking paper and fill with baking weights, dried beans or uncooked rice. Blind bake for 10 minutes, or until the edges begin to turn light golden. Remove the baking paper and weights and cook for a further 10 minutes, until the base is golden. Set aside to cool.

Reduce the oven temperature to 160°C (320°F/Gas 2–3).

To make the filling, using a hand-held blender to cream the butter, sugar and lemon zest together in a medium-sized bowl. Beat the eggs in one at a time. Add the ground almonds and flour and stir to combine.

Spread the jam over the base of the pastry case. Cover with filling and sprinkle with flaked almonds.

Bake for 30–40 minutes, until golden-brown and a skewer comes out clean when tested. Set on a wire rack to cool.

Dust with icing sugar, slice and serve with whipped cream.

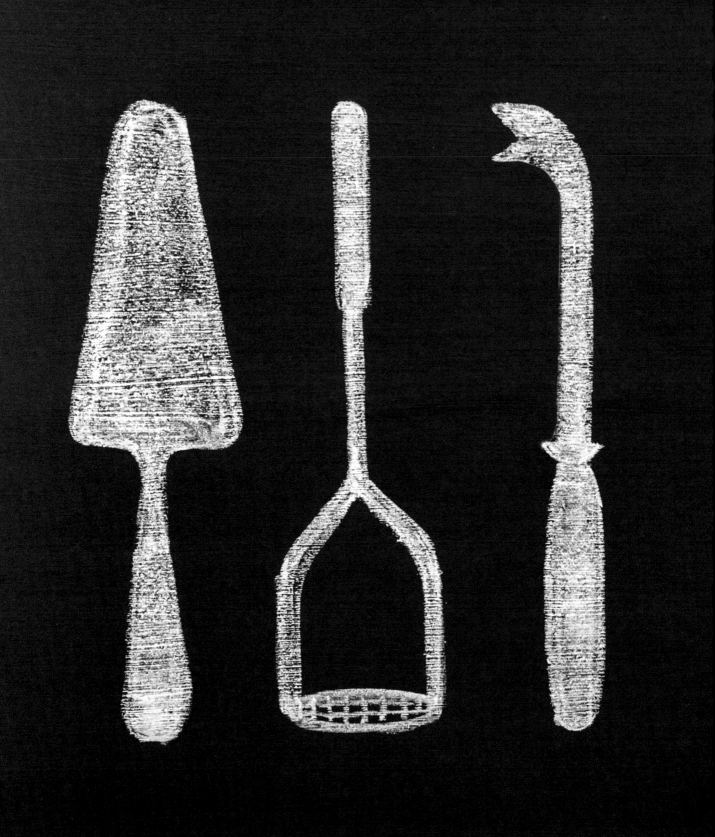

# INDEX

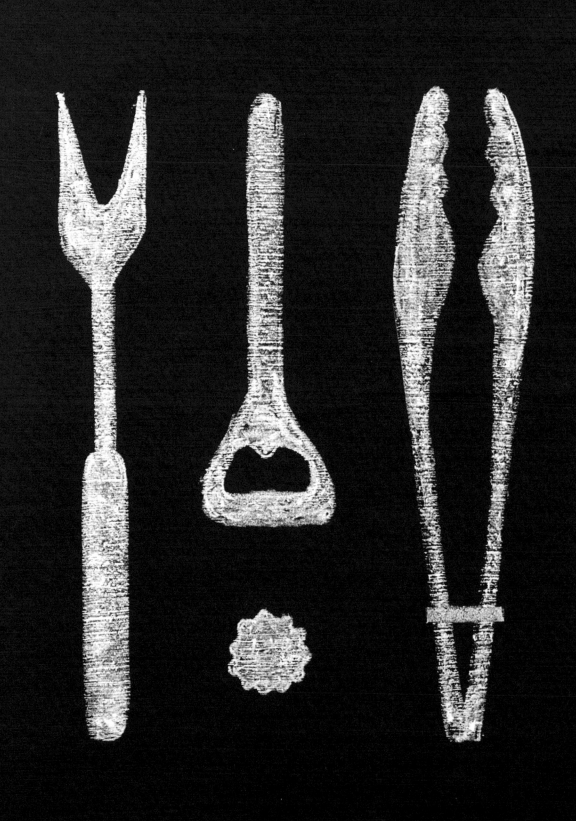

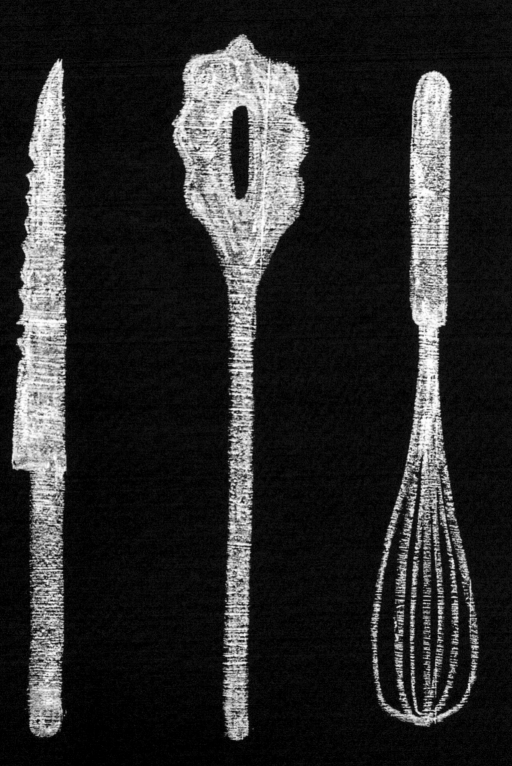

Published in 2012 by Hardie Grant Books

Hardie Grant Books (Australia)
Ground Floor, Building 1
658 Church Street
Richmond, Victoria 3121
www.hardiegrant.com.au

Hardie Grant Books (UK)
Dudley House, North Suite
34–35 Southampton Street
London WC2E 7HF
www.hardiegrant.co.uk

A Cataloguing-in-Publication entry is available
from the catalogue of the National Library of
Australia at www.nla.gov.au

Great Pub Food
ISBN 9781742704517

Publishing Director: Paul McNally
Project Editor: Hannah Koelmeyer
Editor: Clare Coney
Design Manager: Heather Menzies
Designers: Lanz+Martin
Photographer: Lisa Cohen
Stylist: Simon Bajada
Production: Penny Sanderson

Colour reproduction by
Splitting Image Colour Studio

Printed and bound in China by
1010 Printing International Limited